HOLLY CATTERTON ALLEN

Foreword by CATHERINE STONEHOUSE

Forming Resilient Children

The Role of Spiritual Formation
for Healthy Development

Academic
An imprint of InterVarsity Press
Downers Grove, Illinois

InterVarsity Press
P.O. Box 1400, Downers Grove, IL 60515-1426
ivpress.com
email@ivpress.com

InterVarsity Press® is the book-publishing division of InterVarsity Christian Fellowship/USA®, a movement of students and faculty active on campus at hundreds of universities, colleges, and schools of nursing in the United States of America, and a member movement of the International Fellowship of Evangelical Students. For information about local and regional activities, visit intervarsity.org.

All Scripture quotations, unless otherwise indicated, are taken from The Holy Bible, New International Version®, NIV®. Copyright © 1973, 1978, 1984, 2011 by Biblica, Inc.™ Used by permission of Zondervan. All rights reserved worldwide. www.zondervan.com. The "NIV" and "New International Version" are trademarks registered in the United States Patent and Trademark Office by Biblica, Inc.™

While many stories in this book are true, some names and identifying information may have been changed to protect the privacy of individuals.

The publisher cannot verify the accuracy or functionality of website URLs used in this book beyond the date of publication.

Cover design and image composite: Cindy Kiple
Interior design: Daniel van Loon
Images: girl jumping: © Arie Prasetyo / EyeEm / Getty Images
       motion fragments: © Ivcandy / DigitalVision Vectors / Getty Images

ISBN 978-1-5140-0172-1 (print)
ISBN 978-1-5140-0173-8 (digital)

Printed in the United States of America ∞

InterVarsity Press is committed to ecological stewardship and to the conservation of natural resources in all our operations. This book was printed using sustainably sourced paper.

Library of Congress Cataloging-in-Publication Data
A catalog record for this book is available from the Library of Congress.

P	27	26	25	24	23	22	21	20	19	18	17	16	15	14	13	12	11	10	9	8	7	6	5	4	3	2
Y	44	43	42	41	40	39	38	37	36	35	34	33	32	31	30	29	28	27	26	25	24	23	22	21		

"*Forming Resilient Children* is a fresh, honest, and deeply valuable resource for anyone whose work includes the care, mentoring, sheltering, counseling, teaching, adopting, fostering, or parenting of children. True stories enhance the insights, research, and practice that Holly Allen has done so well from Sunday school to university classrooms, from African villages to inner-city America, from the fragility of infants to troubled teens. This book is a valuable guide to helping families, congregations, counselors, and teachers equip children with the resilience needed to live well-shaped lives in a world so often out of shape!"

Robbie F. Castleman, author of *Parenting in the Pew* and professor emerita of theology and New Testament, John Brown University

"A career walking alongside children experiencing hard places has taught me that trauma and grief respect no one. Holly Catterton Allen understands this. She knows that everything in this world is tested, even the faith of children. So she guides us in realistic practices empowering children to shape a faith resilient enough to endure the blowing and beating winds of life. Holly sagely sifts through work from multiple disciplines of scholarship, countless conversations with peers, hundreds of stories from the field, and her own research and experience to give us a model of resilient spiritual formation that works with all children—those living a blessed life and those walking through hard places. This book is a gift of wisdom and hope."

Ron Bruner, executive director of Westview Boys Home, Hollis, Oklahoma

"*Forming Resilient Children* is a much-needed addition to the field of children's spirituality. Especially now, as we continue to face the ongoing effects of a once-a-century pandemic, children need adults who can help them recover from trauma, process grief, and nurture hope. Whether you're a parent, grandparent, pastor, teacher, or children's ministry volunteer, Holly Allen's superb research will help you understand connections between spirituality and resilience. What is more, she offers strategies and resources that you can use to foster resilience among the children that God has placed in your life."

David Csinos, founder of Faith Forward and associate professor of practical theology at Atlantic School of Theology in Halifax, Nova Scotia

"With masterful use of engaging story and sound research, Holly Catterton Allen has given us a thorough and thoughtful exploration into the innate connection between children's spirituality and resilience. She offers practical insights that enable each of us to participate in nurturing resilience in children within the everyday fabric of life where hope and wonder reside. Dr. Allen doesn't avoid the hard topics but gently offers guidance around accompanying children as they process their grief and trauma. *Forming Resilient Children* is the book the world needs right now. Every adult who hopes for good needs to read this book for the good of the children within their circle of influence; our present and future demand it. *Forming Resilient Children* is a book that I will be returning to over and over; I recommend it highly."

Lacy Finn Borgo, spiritual director and author of *Spiritual Conversations with Children: Listening to God Together*

"*Timely!* That's the first word that came to mind when I read this book, given the events of 2020–2021. *Practical!* is the second word. Holly has done a huge service for those who work with children in any setting by providing an extensive resource that connects resilience and spirituality. Acknowledging that all children are spiritual beings is foundational as her starting point for facilitating resilience in children who endure crises of any kind. While recognizing the effect of the pandemic on children, she bookends her work with a powerful story of family resilience while enduring a natural disaster and its aftermath. Well-researched and loaded with stories that put flesh on the guiding principles Holly has developed, *Forming Resilient Children* is a must-have addition to my library of resources focusing on the intrinsic value and capability of children and their families."

Scottie May, associate professor emerita of Christian formation and ministry at Wheaton College, coauthor of *Children Matter*

"Holly Catterton Allen loves children, and it shows in every aspect of her life and work, and especially in this new book, *Forming Resilient Children*. One of the heartbreaking realities of our world today is that there are many children caught in difficult circumstances who experience trauma, loss, and suffering. For so many of us, our desire is to protect them from this reality or distract them from it, hoping they can somehow escape it. This is both foolish and futile. Instead, Holly invites all of us—parents, grandparents, teachers, and others who love and care for children—to learn how to foster and support the kind of spiritual growth and vitality that enables children to hope, lean on God, and persevere in the midst of the hard times that come to us all, young and old. This book is a gift to us all, so I urge you to receive it as such and lend your ears to someone who has much wisdom to share. Your children will thank you for it."

Kevin Lawson, professor of educational studies at Talbot School of Theology, Biola University

"*Forming Resilient Children* shines a bright light toward the need for churches, mentors, and caregivers to partner together to attend to all the places where grief, trauma, and the general struggle of being a human can feel like wading through the darkness for our little ones. Holly Allen brilliantly makes her own research and scholarly work inform the very practical day-to-day conversations we nurture. She provides even more evidence from the field for what we've always intuitively and culturally known to be true: our children need a host of people attending to their spiritual formation."

Jared Boyd, spiritual director and author of *Imaginative Prayer: A Yearlong Guide to Your Child's Spiritual Formation*

"In a field burgeoning with new research, Holly Catterton Allen provides a concise, engaging resource for Christian leaders, parents, and caregivers searching for ways to support the spiritual lives of children in their midst. This book offers a practical guide for Christian leaders to merge findings from the fields of children's spirituality and resilience. Weaving together stories of traumatic events from children's lives, Allen invites the reader to explore the simple but profound ways that support for children's spiritual lives can help them find resilience and hope."

Heather Ingersoll, executive director of Godly Play Foundation in Ashland, Kansas

"Holly Catterton Allen's passion to bridge robust academic research with grounded practical applications immediately surfaces in the first few sentences of the introduction and weaves its way through every page of this book. Further, Holly ties together the various strands of literature from resilience studies, children's spirituality, psychology, sociology, and more to give readers a comprehensive primer on how people who care about children can foster spiritual practices that help children thrive through challenges they may face. The many anecdotes Holly uses from her own personal and academic life as well as from around the world enable the book to speak to international audiences and contexts. As a sociologist interested in how children make meaning of their worlds, I appreciate the way Holly foregrounds children's voices and how she takes every word shared by the children in this book seriously. I highly recommend this book for anyone interested in learning more about the connection between spirituality and resilience, and the real (and surprisingly simple) ways we can connect children to meaning and purpose that can contribute to resilience in the face of difficult times or devastating trauma."

Henry Zonio, director of the Center for Academic Excellence at Asbury University

"Following years of experience and extensive research, Dr. Allen has provided a scholarly and practical guide to assist those who serve with children to create experiences that help them develop resilience. Allen tackles the difficult task of constructing solid definitions of children's spirituality and spiritual formation that are likely to become commonly accepted. Building from these definitions, Allen offers a comprehensive analysis of the many contexts in which resilience can be developed in the lives of children. Her groundbreaking work will have a lasting impact on those who desire to assist children in forming resilience."

Leon M. Blanchette, chair of the department of Christian ministry at Olivet Nazarene University's School of Theology and Christian Ministry

"I wish I had owned this book when my student emailed me. It was the second month of her student teaching semester, the final phase of her teacher preparation program at the university where I serve as the chair of teacher education. 'Dr. K., can we visit? I just want to talk to you about how to respond in healthy and helpful ways to the hard stories my students bring to the classroom.' As a Christian teacher candidate serving in a public school context, it was important to her to nurture children academically, emotionally, and spiritually. Her desire was to provide them with the kind of support that would help them develop healing and hope. But the stories the children brought with them seemed overwhelming. Holly Catterton Allen's book was just the resource she needed. Holly develops a clear and powerful framework based on sound theology and meaningful research. And she provides practical strategies for application in various settings—strategies to support the development of resilience in children recognizing the critical aspect of spirituality. You can be assured I will be sending this book to my former student as she begins her first year of teaching."

Dana Kennamer, associate dean of the College of Education and Human Services, professor and chair of teacher education, Abilene Christian University

"This book is designed for adults who care for children: parents, teachers, pastors, and anyone who desires to support and encourage resilience in the young people in their lives. Using strong research, clear direction, and practical help, Holly Catterton Allen offers valuable guidance to help children address various kinds of significant trauma in their lives and to thrive. An important resource for today and the days yet to come."

Tori Smit, Regional Minister for Faith Formation, Presbyterian Church in Canada

"This is a book filled with poignant accounts of trauma and hope and resilience. The stories in this book brought me to tears at times and also caused me to stop and reflect on my own life and the children within my sphere of influence. But more than these rich stories, this book is simply needed in a world in which resilient people are too often in short supply. It is needed by parents, grandparents, teachers, ministers, and volunteers who engage in the formation process alongside children. Holly Catterton Allen has gifted us with an important book on the effective convergence of resilience and spirituality for such a time as this when, more than ever, children need listening people and spaces to ask questions about God, wonder about their world, and make meaning of their experiences as they live into their own stories and discover their place of belonging in God's story."

Trevecca Okholm, adjunct professor in practical theology at Azusa Pacific University and author of *The Grandparenting Effect: Bridging Generations One Story at a Time*

"What makes this book work so well is the pairing of Holly Allen's interdisciplinary breadth and her ability to root her insights in relatable stories. I'm delighted that the important connection between children's spirituality and resilience has been given such thoughtful and well-informed treatment. This is a really worthwhile addition to literature on children's spirituality."

Rebecca Nye, associate lecturer in childhood studies and child psychology at The Open University, UK, and author of *Children's Spirituality: What It Is and Why It Matters*

"In the 1980s, researchers began to notice the strengths people need to recover from adversity. One critical factor that kept appearing was religion/spirituality. Professor Holly Allen successfully connects the current research of such specialists as Ann Masten and Lisa Miller to the place where ordinary people live. She richly develops what we can do, especially as religious and spiritual people, to give children greater resilience to manage the hardships that confront them. Her book celebrates the seemingly simple but critical practices anyone, including grandparents, can do that support a life of resilience—or may we say, a life of grace."

Jerome Berryman, founder of the Godly Play Foundation and author of *Teaching Godly Play*

"Holly Allen's *Forming Resilient Children* is a necessary and important book that examines the connection between a child's spirituality and resilience. As a significant contribution to the field, this book provides both foundational knowledge as well as practical insights into how parents, grandparents, and ministry leaders can enter into hard places with children and nurture both their resilience and spirituality."

Mimi Larson, visiting assistant professor of Christian formation and ministry at Wheaton College, coeditor of *Bridging Theory and Practice in Children's Spirituality*

This book is dedicated to my children,

David, Daniel, and Bethany,

and to my grandchildren,

Alexandria, Jonathan, Benjamin, Brynna, and Roham,

and to grandchildren and great-grandchildren yet to be born.

My prayer is that you will know the God who

made you and calls you by name,

and that you will live in God's story,

passing on what God teaches you

to the next generation,

and the next.

My people, hear my teaching;
*   listen to the words of my mouth.*
I will open my mouth with a parable;
*   I will utter hidden things, things from of old—*
things we have heard and known,
*   things our ancestors have told us.*
We will not hide them from their descendants;
*   we will tell the next generation*
the praiseworthy deeds of the Lord,
*   his power, and the wonders he has done.*
He decreed statutes for Jacob
*   and established the law in Israel,*
which he commanded our ancestors
*   to teach their children,*
so the next generation would know them,
*   even the children yet to be born,*
*   and they in turn would tell their children.*
Then they would put their trust in God
*   and would not forget his deeds*
*   but would keep his commands.*

Psalm 78:1-7

Contents

Foreword

CATHERINE STONEHOUSE

AS THE GLOBAL CORONAVIRUS PANDEMIC has reminded us, our lives are subject to much uncertainty and stress. We know there is a need to form resilient children, but how can that be done? In this book, Dr. Holly Catterton Allen provides great wisdom and assistance, which comes from her lifelong journey of ministering with children and studying what is best for them. She highlights the importance of the spiritual nurture of children in the forming of resilience.

Dr. Allen began ministering with children at the age of eleven, when her church allowed her to teach a small group of kindergarten children in vacation Bible school. She loved it, and when she entered college several years later, she majored in education. That was followed by a master's degree in educational psychology. She was also active in ministry with children based on her understanding of childhood education.

In the early 1990s the Allen family became a part of an intergenerational small group. Dr. Allen saw children and adults interacting and ministering to one another in meaningful ways. Intergenerational relationships

---

When Dr. Allen asked me to write the foreword for this book, she asked me to give an update to those who would like to know what I have been doing in recent years. Since retiring from Asbury Seminary in 2011, I have continued to receive opportunities to teach about children and their physical, cognitive, socioemotional, and spiritual development. I have spent a few months most years with Asia-Pacific Nazarene Theological Seminary in the Philippines teaching students from around the world who are committed to God's call on their lives. In May 2021, I taught a Zoom course titled "Home and Faith Community: Partners in Transformational Learning." It has also been a privilege to have opportunities to support new books on children's spirituality and to write this foreword.

seemed to provide significant spiritual nurturing for both children and adults. This convinced her there was more to Christian education than cognitive knowledge.

In 1999 Dr. Allen began PhD studies. Her ultimate purpose was to discover what made the difference she had seen in the children, youth, and adults in her intergenerational small group, a difference she had not seen in other settings.

In the 1990s, there was an increase in the number of persons studying and writing about the spirituality of children and how they could be nurtured in that spirituality. These resources were available to the PhD students at that time, and valuable studies are continuing to give new insights.

One of the strengths of this book is the rich literature review and theories related to the forming of resilient children. The theoretical insights come from research by Christians and from the social sciences. And the insights are presented in ways that can be grasped by parents, grandparents, and those who minister with children in the church.

Dr. Allen's theoretical descriptions are understandable as she shares examples from real-life experiences, and she also provides examples of how to apply the theories.

The book is written for a wide range of persons: parents, grandparents, persons leading ministries with children and families in the church, counselors, and those who work in settings where overt spiritual conversations are not allowed. It is a valuable resource for those who desire to raise resilient children to know God and live well in our changing world.

Acknowledgments

I WILL FIRST ACKNOWLEDGE the support I have received from Lipscomb University. I came to Lipscomb a few years ago with a contract in hand from InterVarsity Press for this book. I am deeply appreciative of Lipscomb's gracious offer of a course release each semester for two years to complete this manuscript.

I wish to thank the women with whom I meet and pray on Tuesday evenings: Linda Blanks, Linda Bridgesmith, Mary Hemminger, Rebecca Lavender, and Kathy Musick. We share God's work in us, the work God is calling us to do, the challenges God allows in our lives, and our concerns for our children and our grandchildren, and we encourage each other to go further up and further in.

A small writers' group at Lipscomb has walked with me during the last season of writing this book; this group includes Donita Brown, Tessa Sanders, Leanne Smith, and Denis' Thomas. It is always a rich blessing to listen and learn with fellow writers.

Al Hsu with IVP has been an excellent editor; he has offered insightful suggestions to hone, illustrate, and clarify key points in the book.

Thank you to my friends and children's spirituality colleagues Dana Kennamer, Mimi Larson, Trevecca Okholm, and Robin Turner; they took time from their busy lives to share their favorite children's books that nurture children spiritually (see chapter twelve).

And a big shout-out to my colleague Jason Brian Santos, whose editing skills helped make chapters one and two (the definitional chapters) less formal and more inviting.

Special thanks to the managers and staff at Panera Bread on Old Hickory Boulevard in Brentwood, Tennessee. For the two years (prior to Covid-19) while I composed basic sections of the manuscript and ate broccoli cheddar soup and Caesar salad, these men and women were consistently warm, welcoming, and thoughtful.

To my husband: what a blessing to journey with you for more than four decades, a journey of joy, pain, hope, loss, dreams, disappointments, blessings, and accomplishments. In this season, I thank you for your unfailing support, for your deep belief in me, and for every delicious dinner you prepared—each one was "my favorite."

And finally, I give thanks to God who called me Beloved when I was eleven years old. God saw in me an earnest heart, a child determined to be faithful with a desire to know him before I even knew language to express such a desire. God called me by name and has led me to Christ-followers who know this language and who are now teaching me how to rest in God's long, steady, loving gaze.

Introduction

On Monday, August 29, 2005, Hurricane Katrina overwhelmed the Gulf Coast. It left devastation in its path, especially in New Orleans, where Ruth Walker and her three children—Terrell (age fourteen), James (age eleven), and Jada (age five)—lived in a second-floor apartment in the Seventh Ward. As the city and surrounding areas began to anticipate the approaching disaster, Ruth, a licensed practical nurse, spent much of the weekend helping to evacuate the residents of the nursing home where she worked.

On Sunday morning before she left for the nursing home, Ruth told her son Terrell that they might need to evacuate as well. She asked him to prepare backpacks for himself and his younger brother and sister with a change of clothes (sealed in plastic bags) and two or three special toys or books they wanted to bring. Before she left for work, Ruth prepared a backpack for herself as well as a bag of food and water bottles.

When Ruth arrived home late that night, she woke Terrell and told him they would leave in the morning. The hurricane made landfall on Monday, so Ruth and her family decided to wait out the winds in a large windowless enclosed space on the first floor of the apartment building. In the night, water began seeping into that room, so they went to the second floor to wait till morning. By first light, water was already sloshing onto the steps that led to the second floor as they headed out into driving rain. They began the walk to their friends' house, the Johnsons, whose home was on a slight rise a few blocks away. On the way, Ruth gave the food bag to Terrell and put Jada on her back. The water was rising rapidly, and it was becoming increasingly difficult to avoid stepping into holes or deeper water. The Walkers did not know it, but some of the levees had failed and water from Lake Ponchartrain was flooding into the city. It took two hours to get to the Johnsons' as they detoured around swirling water and avoided flooded streets full of floating debris. When they reached their friends' house, water was inching into the front yard. They ran up the sidewalk and the front steps, where the Johnsons received them, fear etched on their faces.

Over the next several hours, the water climbed the outside steps one by one, then flowed into the house, and from there it began its unstoppable rise to the second floor. As the Johnsons and the Walkers retreated from the first floor, Mrs. Johnson grabbed food, water, candles, and matches from the kitchen.

While the rain beat down steadily, Ruth's family settled into a third-floor storage area while their friends waited in an adjacent room. Terrell and Mr. Johnson watched at the head of the stairs, setting an alarm every hour to gauge the water's rise.

As they changed into dry clothes and wrapped up in blankets, Jada let out a piercing scream: "My dollies! My dollies! I dropped my dollies!" And indeed, her bright-pink backpack was nowhere to be found. The Johnsons came rushing in when Jada began to wail. Ruth held Jada, comforted her, and rocked her, singing all the favorite lullabies she had sung when Jada was a baby. Gradually Jada calmed down, and everybody sat on the floor looking at each other.

Then James said in a tremulous voice, "God promised he wouldn't ever flood the whole earth again, didn't he?"

Everyone laughed a bit, and they decided to retell the Noah story. At the end, Jada and the twin Johnson girls were asleep, and James said, "There were eight people in the ark and there are eight of us here." They thanked God for preserving their lives in this "ark" and then began to figure out how they might sleep.

In the night, the water rose almost to the third floor, and as morning came they began to consider how to leave the house for a safer place.

Terrell and Mr. Johnson managed to get a window open, and they surveyed the scene just below the window. Rowboats and canoes were making their way across the canals that used to be their neighborhood streets. When James looked out the window, he turned to his mom and asked anxiously, "Are we going to get out of here?"

Ruth replied with conviction, "Of course we are, James. God has brought us this far; one of those boats will carry us to the next stop on our journey."

Around midafternoon, Mr. Johnson's brother came for them in a boat. First, he rowed Ruth and her children to a church in a higher part of the city that had sustained less hurricane damage, then he went back for his brother's family.

The Walkers received food and water, and they slept in a large room with dozens of other survivors. Jada slept poorly and woke often, crying and asking about her dollies. Terrell was attentive to the needs of his sister and brother and did whatever his mother needed him to do. James asked questions: "Why did this happen to us? Will we get to go back to our place? Will it be there? Will our stuff be there? Will we get to start school? Will my soccer team still get to play our games?"

Ruth answered as best as she could. She was exhausted and worried.

Over the next few days, Ruth began to understand that the Seventh Ward—indeed much of New Orleans—would not recover in a few weeks, and she began to consider where her family should go. When buses heading for Arkansas arrived, she and her family climbed aboard, first arriving in Fort Chaffee, then on to Siloam Springs, arriving Labor Day weekend. Along with about seven hundred other hurricane refugees, they were taken to a now-empty summer camp that had been prepared for their arrival.

A hundred and fifty Siloam volunteers prepared meals, set up communication stations for the evacuees to call their families, and took people to the doctor, the pharmacy, and Walmart. They listened to stories of fear and loss.

For Ruth and her family, life began to take shape. For the moment, food and shelter were provided and volunteers had found clothing from Goodwill for everyone in the family. Ruth registered her children in Siloam Springs schools, and she began seeking a job as an LPN. Within two weeks she had secured a position at a local nursing home, and since the camp would close at the end of October (as the buildings were not heated), Ruth began looking for an apartment for her family.

James asked, "Are we going back to New Orleans? Will I get to go back to my real school? I want to play soccer; can I join a team here till we go back?"

Terrell said, "Maybe we should get an apartment on the third floor."

Soon after they arrived in Siloam, Ruth's family began worshiping at a vibrant community church along with some of the other hurricane evacuees. The church welcomed them with warmth and joy, offering support in any way that was needed. In November, the family moved into a *third-floor*, two-bedroom apartment that had been filled with furniture by church members. Someone even provided a serviceable 1995 Honda Civic.

Terrell was befriended by a couple of guys in the youth group who were on the middle school football team, and the coaches welcomed the new kids from New Orleans. James joined a soccer team, and Ruth began to sing in the church choir. Jada seemed withdrawn and anxious.

When Ruth picked up Jada from kindergarten each day, the little girl seemed troubled. Ruth spoke with Jada's teacher, who showed her Jada's drawings. They were drawn with gray, black, brown, and dark blue crayons; they showed rain, broken houses, water, and boats. In every picture, Jada drew her dollies in the water.

One night when Ruth was tucking Jada into bed, Jada asked in a tremulous voice, "Where are my dollies?"

Ruth wasn't sure what to say. They prayed as they always did, thanking God for saving them from the storm, but on this night, Jada asked God to find her dollies and bring them back to her.

By Thanksgiving about two hundred and fifty people from New Orleans remained in Siloam. Many of these families came together to give thanks for their safety and for this new place. It was good to hear each other's stories from the hurricane, as well as accounts of how the various families were making their way in Siloam Springs.

James told everyone his family was moving back to New Orleans as soon as they could, which surprised Ruth since they had not discussed this possibility. Terrell stayed near his mom and told everyone that everything was really great. Jada said little.

When the family got back to their apartment, Ruth called a family meeting. She asked Terrell if everything really was okay, and he said it was—but Ruth suspected that he might be saying he was okay so she wouldn't worry. She asked James if he thought the family was going to move back to New Orleans, and he said, "Of course we are; it's our home." Ruth asked Jada how her brand-new dollies were doing, and Jada said, "They're okay. I'm taking good care of them," but her face was bleak.

Then Terrell asked his mom how she was doing. She said, "I think I'm all right, but I'm not sure we should move back to New Orleans."

James immediately yelled, "Why not? Nobody ever listens to me!" And with that he stormed out of the room.

That night Ruth realized she needed help and that her children needed help.

We will return to the story of the Walker family in the conclusion of this book. We will see how this family navigates the next stages of their journey. Ruth, Terrell, James, and Jada lean into the spiritual processes shared in the pages ahead, and each one offers a portrait of resilience that is encouraging and memorable.

• • •

Interest in the topic of resilience seems to rise in difficult times. Without question, the twenty-first century—with its numerous natural disasters, wars, pandemics (including the coronavirus), and political and economic crises—is proving to be a very difficult time. The well-being of children is threatened by these same upheavals as well as by other sufferings such as poverty, neglect, and abuse. Since it is impossible to protect children from all adversity and hardship in life, resilience research explores ways to promote healthy development in children in all circumstances. In the past, resilience literature has tended to overlook or downplay the key role of spirituality (though it has sometimes given credence to the role of religion).[1] In the last two decades, however, psychologists such as

---

[1]Chapter two discusses the similarities and differences regarding spirituality and religion.

Ann Masten[2] and Lisa Miller[3] have been constructing a strong case for the interconnection between resilience and spirituality.

This book seeks to build a bridge from the broader field of resilience to the place where ordinary people live. It is written for all who want to understand how spirituality and resilience are connected and who want to foster resilience in children, whether as academics or practitioners. It is for everyone who recognizes that children need resilience to manage the ordinary difficulties in their lives as well as the more significant hardships that may come. The book is for those who work with children in every circumstance—children who live in poverty, who are refugees, who are coping with asthma or diabetes, who have a sibling with special needs, or whose parents are divorcing. Anyone who spends time with children regularly eventually sees some who are struggling in one or more of these circumstances, and it is clear that for these children to flourish, they will need to be resilient.

The study of resilience is an emerging field that once focused primarily on those who had overcome severe hardship but now recognizes that all children need to be resilient, since facing trials and setbacks is a universal experience. Psychologists describe resilience as the process of adapting well in the face of adversity, trauma, or significant sources of stress.[4]

All children need to be able to deal with stress, cope with challenges, and persevere through disappointment. How do children learn to cope and persevere? Resilience literature describes multiple factors that can

---

[2]Ann Masten, PhD, is a professor at the Institute for Child Development at the University of Minnesota known for her research on the development of resilience and for advancing theory on the positive outcomes of children and families facing adversity. Masten received the American Psychological Association Urie Bronfenbrenner Award for Lifetime Contributions to the Service of Science and Society in 2014. She has served as president of the Society for Research in Child Development and of Division Seven (Developmental) of the American Psychological Association.

[3]Lisa Miller, PhD, is a professor, researcher, and clinical psychologist best known for her research on spirituality in psychology. Miller is director of clinical psychology and founder of the Spirituality Mind Body Institute at Columbia University Teachers College. Miller is coeditor in chief of *Spirituality in Clinical Practice* published by the American Psychological Association, the first peer-reviewed academic journal dedicated to spirituality as a source of healing and growth in treatment and well-being work.

[4]"Building Your Resilience," American Psychological Association, 2012, www.apa.org/topics /resilience.

generate resilience in children, and recently several researchers have begun exploring spirituality as one of those factors.[5]

The study of children's spirituality is an emerging cross-disciplinary field. When exploring spirituality religiously and nonreligiously, psychologists, sociologists, theologians, child development specialists, pedagogical experts, and spiritual formation leaders all bring important perspectives to the table.

A key tenet of children's spirituality studies is that children are spiritual beings. Though parents and those who work with children tend to agree with this assertion, Western culture in general has not been welcoming to spirituality. In fact, most children, though they may experience a strong sense of transcendence, realize that talking about spiritual matters is socially unacceptable in general. Children's spirituality experts David Hay and Rebecca Nye note that the children in their study (ages six to eleven) were already aware that there is a "social taboo" regarding speaking about spirituality.[6]

Rebecca Nye found that this social taboo was present in higher education as well: "I was advised by the first professor of psychology I worked for that it would be 'academic suicide' to research the psychology of children's spirituality as a Ph.D. topic."[7] Lisa Miller found this to be so as well. When she began her research as a clinical psychologist around 2000, she encountered a strong bias in the social and medical sciences against research on spirituality.

Miller attributes the skepticism and bias she faced to the fact that most twentieth-century psychologists operated primarily out of a secular materialist worldview—that is, a worldview that holds that all things are composed of the material and that spiritual realities, if they exist, are irrelevant. In the *Oxford University Press Handbook of Psychology and*

---

[5]A number of terms or phrases are used for this factor, including faith, spiritual support, belief that life has meaning, and hope.

[6]David Hay with Rebecca Nye, *The Spirit of the Child*, rev. ed. (London: Jessica Kingsley Publishers, 2006), 132.

[7]Rebecca Nye, "Back Page Interview: Rebecca Nye, Child Psychologist," *Church Times*, May 13, 2009, www.churchtimes.co.uk/articles/2009/15-may/features/back-page-interview-rebecca-nye child-psychologist.

Spirituality, Miller chronicles the changes of the past few decades as psychologists (and others in academia) have begun to make room for the idea that there is more to reality than reason and the senses, and that there are, in fact, spiritual realities to assimilate into a holistic understanding of the world and those who live in it.[8] Miller notes that the authors of the forty chapters in the handbook see spirituality as a fundamental human quality and a foundational aspect of the universe.[9]

All this to say, research about spirituality in the social sciences is now more acceptable than it was in the past. Unfortunately, biases from the twentieth century run deep; consequently, children and youth typically receive little support from schools, communities, or even parents to develop their inherent spirituality.

Miller has spent the last twenty years researching the idea of spiritual strength as a source of coping and resilience especially for children and youth. Her findings as well as the results of other studies offer a new science of spirituality and thriving.[10] This book, *Forming Resilient Children*, builds a bridge between recent resilience studies and children's spirituality so that parents, teachers, ministers, social workers, counselors, and community caregivers can give the spiritual support children and adolescents need to thrive in these challenging times.

OVERVIEW OF THE BOOK

Here is a road map of the journey we will take together in looking at children's resilience and spirituality.

Part one. Chapters one, two, and three lay the foundation for the premise of this book—that nurturing spirituality in children promotes resilience. To make this book applicable both in Christian settings and in secular environments where Christians work, chapter one constructs a general definition of children's spirituality as well as a specific definition of children's spiritual formation from a Christian perspective.

---

[8]Lisa Miller, "Introduction," in *Oxford University Press Handbook of Psychology and Spirituality*, ed. Lisa Miller (New York: Oxford University Press, 2012), 1.

[9]Miller, "Introduction."

[10]Lisa Miller, *The Spiritual Child: The New Science on Parenting for Health and Lifelong Thriving* (New York: St. Martin's Press, 2015).

Chapter two then offers usable, lay-friendly definitions of resilience and summarizes the current conversation around various factors that contribute to resilience. And chapter three furthers the discussion, nuancing the interconnections between spirituality and resilience.

Part two. Parents are keenly aware that one of their tasks is to prepare their children to survive in a world fraught with unforeseeable challenges. Chapter four endeavors to equip parents who are seeking effective ways to foster resilience in their children. Chapter five extends this support to grandparents, describing how they can nurture their grandchildren through their intentional involvement in their lives.

Part three. Chapters six, seven, eight, and nine share multiple ways resilience can be cultivated in Christian settings, including intergenerational faith communities and in Sunday school through leaning into God's story, into body-spirit connections, and into wonder.

Part four. Chapters ten, eleven, and twelve address the needs of children who have already experienced severe adversity, such as trauma, deep grief, or painful loss. It is written especially for those who work with children in secular settings—that is, Christians who want to nurture spirituality in the children with whom they work in public settings. They are keenly aware that these children need every physical, intellectual, psychological, emotional, social, and spiritual resource available to them to survive and to thrive.

Conclusion. Chapter thirteen highlights the role of that most necessary spiritual quality—hope. And the epilogue concludes the Walker family's narrative, linking spirituality and resilience in their story of hardship and survival.

Children have an innate, God-bestowed spirituality that is their greatest source of resilience.[11] However, they need adults to come around them and support that intrinsic spiritual quality. This book will focus on ways adults can nurture children spiritually in order to assist them in their spiritual and religious lives in becoming resilient as they cope with current circumstances and to prepare them for unexpected hardships that may come their way.

---

[11]Miller, *Spiritual Child.*

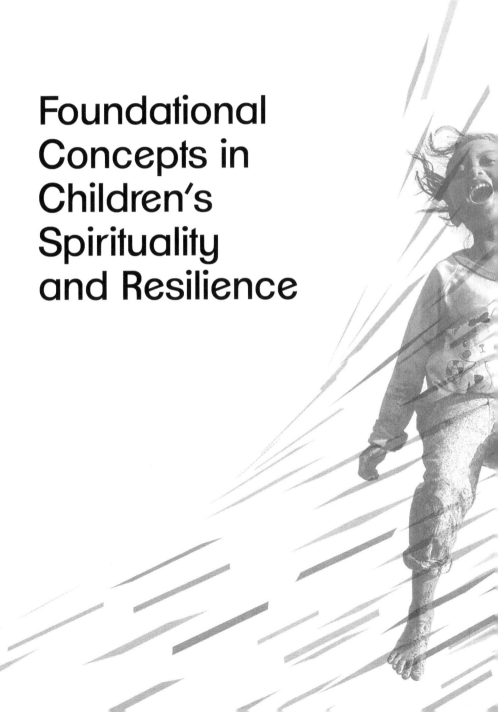

PART ONE

Foundational Concepts in Children's Spirituality and Resilience

CHAPTER ONE

What Is Children's Spirituality?

We are not human beings having a spiritual experience, we
are spiritual beings having a human experience.

PIERRE TEILHARD DE CHARDIN

IN THE SUMMER OF 2019, our three-month-old grandson, Roham, experienced a seizure in his sleep that caused him to vomit, then aspirate the vomitus into his lungs, prompting a critical medical crisis. After repeatedly performing interventions to address the problems that were threatening his life—a racing heart, plummeting blood pressure, low oxygen levels, precipitous carbon dioxide levels, and undulating body temperature—doctors eventually stabilized him and sedated him as they inserted the ventilator tube to help him breathe.

This previously vibrant, active infant remained eerily still—passive, immobile, unconscious—for five days. When the danger finally receded, the doctors began to remove the tubes. As they brought him out of sedation, Roham was desperately unhappy, attempting to cry (though he had lost his voice), nurse (though his throat was too sore to swallow), and sleep (though he was too utterly wretched to do so) for a day and a half—that felt like an eternity. He did nothing but sit upright on his mother's lap for thirty-six hours straight. He sat facing forward (to accommodate the monitoring wires attached to his chest), peering out solemnly in desperation. He refused to be put down. Nor did he smile or engage in any other way.

His only comfort appeared to be gripping one of his mother's fingers in each of his tiny hands while sitting in her warm lap. Roham was navigating not only a physical crisis, but a spiritual crisis as well—as we shall see.

INITIAL INTEREST IN CHILDREN'S SPIRITUALITY

Something happened in the 1990s that dramatically altered my understanding of faith development in children. With a master's degree in educational psychology from the University of Iowa, fifteen years as a professor of teacher education at two Christian universities, and a couple of decades of teaching Sunday school and leading children's church following an educational model, I was confident that I understood the basic principles of Christian education. Then something happened that radically reoriented my thinking about children and faith.

For four years in the midnineties my family was part of a church plant that met each Sunday evening in cross-generational home gatherings. Every week we participated in these small groups—eating, praying, listening, laughing, sharing, and hoping—with all ages participating together. During this time, I began to experience something I had not seen in my years teaching Sunday school and leading children's church: the children in these all-age small groups began to pray with and for their parents and other adults; they began to minister to each other and to adults as well. My understanding of Christian education for both children and adults began to change, and ultimately, my new understandings led me to embrace a career shift.

In 1999 my family and I left West Texas for California, where I pursued doctoral work with one burning question in mind: What might explain the profound effects I and my family had observed and experienced in those intergenerational small groups? My hope was to understand the impact of intergenerational Christian experiences on children (and adults); however, before I could delve into that central question, I needed to understand the nature of the change I had witnessed.

Just one year earlier, Catherine Stonehouse's *Joining Children on the Spiritual Journey* was published.[1] Her book first gave me language for

---

[1] Catherine Stonehouse, *Joining Children on the Spiritual Journey: Nurturing a Life of Faith* (Grand Rapids, MI: Baker Books, 1998).

my task: the basic construct I was exploring was "spirituality." Thus I began a twenty-year (and ongoing) quest to define and describe—that is, to understand—children's spirituality.

The premise of this book is that resilience in children is interconnected with spirituality. To unpack this premise, we'll first need a rich understanding of spirituality, beginning with the idea that spirituality is an innate universal human quality. From this vantage point, I'll establish a working definition of children's spirituality.

SPIRITUALITY AS A UNIVERSAL HUMAN QUALITY

Researchers in the past two decades have been exploring the idea that spirituality is a universal human quality.[2] For example, biologist Dean Hamer believes faith is hardwired into our genes, though he doesn't mean by that statement that there is a particular gene that makes people believe in God. Rather he believes that human beings are predisposed to be spiritual, to seek a higher being.[3]

Before these more general studies on spirituality, Barbara Kimes Myers in the United States and David Hay in the United Kingdom conducted groundbreaking research in the area of children's spirituality. Myers and Hay, both working from Christian worldviews, spent their long, successful careers speaking primarily into secular educational settings, along the way seeking ways for children's spirituality to be fostered in these public education settings.

Myers' greatest contribution has been in the area of preschool education. Myers explains spirituality as an inherent part of the condition of being human, noting that all human beings have spirit as a "life-giving force."[4]

---

[2]See, e.g., Justin Barrett, *Born Believers: The Science of Children's Religious Belief* (Free Press, 2012); R. L. Piedmont, "Cross-cultural Generalizability of the Spiritual Transcendence Scale to the Philippines: Spirituality as a Human Universal," *Mental Health, Religion, and Culture* 10 (2007): 89-107; T. E. Seeman, L. F. Dubin, and M. Seeman, "Religiosity/Spirituality and Health: A Critical Review of the Evidence for Biological Pathways," *American Psychologist* 58, no. 1 (2003): 53-63; R. L. Piedmont, "Does Spirituality Represent the Sixth Factor of Personality? Spiritual Transcendence and the Five Factor Model," *Journal of Personality* 67 (1999): 985-1013.
[3]Dean Hamer, *The God Gene: How Faith Is Hardwired into Our Genes* (New York: Anchor Books, 2005); Dean Hamer, "The Brain Chemistry of the Buddha," BeliefNet, 2004, www.beliefnet.com /news/science-religion/2004/10/the-brain-chemistry-of-the-buddha.aspx.
[4]Barbara Kimes Myers, *Young Children and Spirituality* (New York: Routledge, 1997), 109.

David Hay is well known for his now-classic book (with Rebecca Nye) *The Spirit of the Child*.[5] Hay and Nye conducted exploratory research with children ages six to eleven in the British public school system in order to address two issues that trouble the study of children's spirituality: (1) a lack of consensus on what spirituality is, and (2) a scarcity of specific details regarding the spiritual life of children.[6] The foundational premise of their book is that every person possesses spiritual awareness.[7]

And Lisa Miller, who has spent much of her career as a psychologist and clinician researching spiritual psychology, agrees that children are born with a natural spirituality. She says it is foundational to who we are as human beings.[8]

Hamer, Myers, Hay, Nye, Miller, and many others argue that human beings, even before receiving any formal religious training, possess a spiritual awareness that can be cultivated—or hindered.

A WORKING DEFINITION OF CHILDREN'S SPIRITUALITY

Building directly on this idea that children are spiritual beings from birth, my desire is to construct a definition of children's spirituality that will be suitable and beneficial to anyone who picks up this book. Those who live or work with children in Christian settings may desire a definition that encompasses an explicitly Christian perspective.[9] However, for many believers working with children in government and other secular settings, a Christ-focused definition of children's spirituality would be problematic. Nevertheless, these workers are aware that children, especially those navigating hard places, need every physical, intellectual, emotional, social, and *spiritual* resource available to help them survive and thrive. Nevertheless, these concerned teachers, social workers, and counselors therefore need a broad definition of children's spirituality that will help children access those spiritual resources.

---

[5]David Hay with Rebecca Nye, *The Spirit of the Child*, rev. ed. (London: Jessica Kingsley Publishers, 2006). Original edition published in 1998.
[6]Hay, *Spirit of the Child*, 9.
[7]Hay, *Spirit of the Child*.
[8]Miller, *The Spiritual Child*, 54.
[9]I offer an explicitly Christian definition later in this chapter.

Definitions of spirituality abound. They sometimes refer ambiguously to some inner quality or to participation in a project greater than one-self.[10] Other definitions include references to making meaning, being aware of mystery or wonder, or existential realities. Many definitions refer to the importance of relationality, in particular, relationships with self, with others, with the world, and with God (or a transcendent being). A few definitions focus specifically on children, and these definitions tend to emphasize relationality. For example, Myers defines children's spirituality as a web of meaning "connecting self, others, world, and cosmos."[11] And Hay and Nye define children's spirituality as *relational consciousness*, which they describe as children's understanding of how they relate to other people, to self, to things, and to God.[12] Lisa Miller's definition of spirituality initially focuses on the child-God relationship, but then she broadens it saying spirituality is experienced with *one another*, with a *higher power*, and *within ourselves*,[13] thus aligning fairly closely with the relational definitions of Hay and Myers.

Three relationships, the person's relationship with self, others, and God (or higher being), appear frequently in definitions of children's spirituality[14] as well as definitions of spirituality in general. For example, John Swinton, an expert on spirituality and mental health challenges, frames his definition of spirituality using the terms *interpersonal*,

[10]Kenneth J. Collins, ed., *Exploring Christian Spirituality: An Ecumenical Reader* (Grand Rapids, MI: Baker Book House, 2000), 10.

[11]Myers, *Young Children,* 101.

[12]Hay, *Spirit of the Child,* 109. Early in their research, Hay and Nye had hoped their research would yield a definition of children's spirituality that did not refer to God per se, a definition that could more readily be embraced by atheists and agnostics (Hay, *Spirit of the Child,* 21). The children in their research, however, almost unanimously referred to the idea of a transcendent or super-natural being as God—even though over half of the research participants identified as having no religion. Of the thirty-eight children in the Hay and Nye study, twenty-eight were not affili-ated with a religion. Four of the thirty-eight children were from the Church of England, four were Muslim, and two were Catholic. All attended public schools in either Nottingham or Bir-mingham (UK) (Hay, *Spirit of the Child,* 87).

[13]Miller, *The Spiritual Child,* 52.

[14]Some definitions also include the person-world (or person-universe) relationship as an aspect of spirituality. Though it is not a focal point in this book, I acknowledge that the child-world relationship can indeed play a vital role in children's spirituality and I discuss this relationship in chapter nine on wonder.

intrapersonal, and *transpersonal* which reflect precisely the three dimensions we are discussing.[15]

Our broad definition of children's spirituality will focus principally on these three relationships—the child-self, child-others, and child-God relationships—not only because of their frequent appearance in definitions but also because these three relationships reflect the first and second commandments: "You shall love the Lord your God with all your heart and with all your soul and with all your strength and with all your mind, and your neighbor as yourself" (Luke 10:27 ESV).

Therefore, I offer the following as our working definition of children's spirituality: *children's spirituality is a quality present in every child from birth by which children seek to establish relationship with self, others, and God (as they understand God).*

This definition works for all settings: homes, churches, counseling sessions, social work settings, public schools—everywhere. In addition, it offers a basic foundation for nurturing the inborn human quality of spirituality that aids resilience.

CHILDREN'S SPIRITUALITY AS SPIRITUAL FORMATION FROM A CHRISTIAN PERSPECTIVE

Those who work in Christian settings such as churches, schools, seminaries, and faith-based nonprofits may desire an explicitly Christian definition of children's spirituality. That definition needs to begin with our working definition shared earlier: the child's inborn capability for relationship with self, others, and God.

This basic definition offers correctives to two misconceptions that have characterized some approaches to Christian education. First, some have asserted that a child's spiritual life begins only when the child is baptized (as an infant or older) or invites Jesus into his or her heart. Viewing spirituality (in this case, the child's relationship with God) as beginning at this time leaves children in an ambiguous place for the first several

---

[15]John Swinton, *Spirituality and Mental Health Care: Rediscovering a "Forgotten" Dimension* (Philadelphia: Jessica Kingsley Publishers, 2001).

weeks, months, or years of life. If the child-God relationship begins only at this point, how can parents or teachers nurture it before it exists?

Another misconception is that Christ-followers sometimes view a child's spiritual life as pertaining only to the child-God relationship, not recognizing that the child's relationships with self and others are also integral parts of the spiritual life. As we have seen, children's spirituality is a holistic quality interconnected with all aspects of the child's life, and so this forms the first foundational piece of our definition of children's spirituality from a Christian perspective: the child's relationship with God, self, others.

Christian spirituality. To begin to construct a comprehensive usable definition of spirituality from an explicitly Christian perspective, we will first consult several strong definitions. For my dissertation I combed dozens of sources and considered over a hundred definitions. Three definitions have stood the test of time for me. One comes from Jesuit Sandra Schneiders. Her beautiful and succinct definition of Christian spirituality is "the substantial gift of the Holy Spirit establishing a life-giving relationship with God in Christ within the believing community."[16] Another comes from British theologian Philip Sheldrake who states that Christian spirituality is "a conscious relationship with God, in Jesus Christ, through the indwelling of the Spirit and in the context of community of believers."[17]

These two definitions capture three key concepts often found in definitions of Christian spirituality: (1) they have a trinitarian focus (God the Father, God the Son, and God the Holy Spirit), (2) they emphasize relationality (already present in our first broad definition), and (3) they both acknowledge the important role of a believing community.

The third definition comes from Thomas Groome, a well-known Catholic religious educator. His definition highlights the crucial idea that

---

[16]Sandra Schneiders, "Theology and Spirituality: Strangers, Rivals, and Partners," *Horizon* 13 (1986): 266.

[17]Philip Sheldrake, "What Is Spirituality?" in *Exploring Christian Spirituality*, ed. Kenneth J. Collins (Grand Rapids, MI: Baker Book House, 2000), 40.

Christian spirituality is not solely an interior quality; that is, it will ultimately show in a person's life:

> Spirituality is our conscious attending to God's loving initiative and presence in our lives and to the movement of God's spirit to commit ourselves to wholeness for ourselves and for all humankind *by living in right relationship with God, ourselves, and others in every dimension and activity of our lives.*[18]

Some would call this evidence spiritual fruit.

Therefore, to our original aspects (child's relationship with self, others, and God), we add several more aspects: God as trinitarian, the significant role of a community of believers, and spiritual fruit.

Christian spiritual formation. Another line of investigation from which to draw is spiritual formation. The term "spiritual formation" began to be increasingly and broadly used in Protestant Christian circles in the 1990s to describe the believer's journey of growth and sanctification, though the phrase is deeply rooted in the Catholic tradition.

Professor and author Robert Mulholland's description is one of the most frequently cited definitions: "Spiritual formation is a process of being formed in the image of Christ for the sake of others."[19] Key words and phrases like "process," "formed," "image of Christ," and "for the sake of others" from Mulholland's statement are central to our understanding of our definition of Christian spirituality.

Moreover, James Wilhoit, professor of Christian formation and spirituality at Wheaton College for decades, adds to our developing definition by describing Christian spiritual formation as "the intentional communal process of growing in our relationship with God and becoming conformed to Christ through the power of the Holy Spirit."[20] Beyond reflecting Mulholland's notions of "process" and "being formed," two unique words from Wilhoit's definition emerge as important: "intentional" and "communal."

---

[18]Thomas Groome, "The Spirituality of the Religious Educator," *Religious Education* 83 (1988): 10, emphasis added.

[19]M. Robert Mulholland, *Invitation to a Journey: A Road Map for Spiritual Formation*, exp. ed. (Downers Grove, IL: InterVarsity Press, 2016), 16.

[20]James Wilhoit, *Spiritual Formation as if the Church Mattered: Growing in Christ Through Community* (Grand Rapids, MI: Baker Academic, 2008), 23.

A WORKING DEFINITION OF CHILDREN'S SPIRITUALITY FROM A CHRISTIAN PERSPECTIVE

For years, I have attempted to create a comprehensive working definition that incorporates the eleven key phrases in the preceding discussion of children's spirituality, Christian spirituality, and spiritual formation: *relationship* with *self, others, and God (Father, Son,* and *Holy Spirit); process; role of believing community (communal); spiritual fruit; intentionality;* and *transformation (into Christ's image).*

During these same years I have been teaching university courses and speaking in churches, academic guilds, and church-based conferences on children's ministry, intergenerational ministry, and children's spirituality. In each of these settings I have invited students and conference participants to construct a working definition that incorporates all eleven terms and concepts outlined above. In reviewing dozens of good attempts over the years, two stood out as excellent. I have integrated these two, tweaking and altering a few words, and here, for the first time in print, is the definition I now share wherever I speak:

> Spiritual formation is a lifelong, intentional, communal process of growing more aware of God's presence and becoming more like Christ, through the Spirit, in order to live in restored relationship with God, ourselves, and others, in every dimension of life.[21]

Importantly, this definition is not unique to children; it is a good definition of spiritual formation from a Christian perspective for anyone.

CONCLUSION

The spiritual nature of children has been a neglected topic in both secular and Christian settings—for different reasons of course. Public institutions in the United States including schools,[22] have typically avoided language that refers to the spiritual lives of children because doing so could be construed as promoting a particular religion. This chapter therefore

---

[21]This definition builds on the previous discussion and blends and modifies definitions from Ryan Porche (small groups minister at Southwest Church of Christ in Amarillo, Texas) and Doug Williams and the spiritual life committee at Lipscomb Academy in Nashville, Tennessee.

[22]Joan Montgomery Halford, "Longing for the Sacred in Schools: A Conversation with Nel Noddings," *The Spirit of Education* 56, no. 4 (December 1998/January 1999): 28-32.

offers a definition of children's spirituality that can be used in any setting—*a quality present in every child from birth out of which children seek to establish relationship with self, others, and God (as they understand God)*. This definition provides common ground for cross-disciplinary, as well as cross-denominational and interfaith, dialogue to flourish.

And the definition of children's spirituality from an overtly Christian perspective incorporates the essence of our working definition—those three relationships—while providing a robust, layered version of children's spirituality that will expand and amplify the understanding of ministry with children in specifically Christian settings.

Throughout the remainder of this book, I will focus primarily on these three relationships—the child-self, child-others, and child-God relationships. Additionally, I will outline and describe dozens of ways teachers, caregivers, parents, counselors, social workers, grandparents, psychologists, and medical professionals can nurture this ineffable quality of spirituality (these three relationships) in the children in their care—with a special emphasis on how it contributes to that other mysterious quality of resilience.

BACK TO ROHAM'S STORY

In those hours of recovery as Roham slowly emerged from his necessary dependence on fentanyl, his main comfort appeared to be holding onto his mother's fingers. Humans are clearly made for relationship; this tiny little one held onto life and hope by holding onto his mother.

And then . . . after thirty-six hours, Roham smiled and began to come back to us.

Being physically present is one way to nurture a child spiritually, one way to foster resilience. In this physical connection, children come to know that they are not alone, that someone is with them, supporting, comforting, accompanying.[23] This physical connection fosters the child-self and child-others parts of children's spirituality, which sets a good foundation for nurturing the ineffable child-God relationship.

---

[23]Ruth Feldman, Zehava Rosenthal, and Arthur I. Eidelman, "Maternal-Preterm Skin-to-Skin Contact Enhances Child Physiologic Organization and Cognitive Control Across the First 10 Years of Life," *Biological Psychiatry* 75, no. 1 (2014): 56-64.

CHAPTER TWO

Resilience in Children

MIGUEL[1] IS ONE OF THE CHILDREN *who survived the Sandy Hook Elementary School shooting in 2012. The shooter entered Miguel's first grade classroom, paused, then shot the teacher and one of Miguel's classmates. While the shooter was reloading, Miguel and other children ran out of the building, past the bodies of their principal and others who had been shot. Miguel heard most of the 156 shots fired that day. Since that time, Miguel has asked about his friends who were killed, and sometimes he dreams about that terrible day.*[2]

Many children around the world are involved in traumatic situations. In recent memory, children have survived population-wide traumas such as Hurricane Katrina in 2005 and the earthquake in Haiti in 2010. Some children have lived through civil wars and become refugees, suffering food shortages, poor medical care, inadequate shelter, and the fear of an unknown future.

Other children have watched a parent be taken into custody. Some have endured ongoing personal or family traumas such as parental addictions or mental illness, chronically violent neighborhoods, or physical or sexual abuse.

Parts of this chapter were adapted from Holly Catterton Allen, "Resilience, Trauma, and Children's Spirituality" (with Lipscomb students Kaylee Frank and Megan Larry) in *Bridging Theory and Practice in Children's Spirituality*, ed. Mimi Larson and Robert Keeley (Grand Rapids, MI: Zondervan, 2020), 127-43. Used by permission of Zondervan, www.zondervan.com.
[1]Miguel is a pseudonym; in the press this boy's last name is identified as Rojas.
[2]Associated Press, "'I Know Where the Bad Guy Is': Parents Reveal the Terrible Nightmares of Sandy Hook Survivors," *Daily Mail*, September 29, 2013, www.dailymail.co.uk/news/article-2437438 /children-survived-sandy-hook-massacre-live-in-terror-endure-frequent-nightmares.html.

Of course, many children live whole childhoods without facing traumatic situations such as those described above. Nevertheless, most children encounter some type of troubling issue in childhood such as parental divorce, bullying, chronic childhood illness, a sport-ending athletic injury, rejection from a friend group, academic failure, or the death of a grandparent.

Some children come through difficult circumstances remarkably well, overcoming even severe adversity, while other children remain fragile into adulthood. For example, former child soldiers such as Ishmael Beah have chronicled their extraordinary resilience,[3] while other children grow up processing and reprocessing an episode of bullying from their middle school years that continues to profoundly affect their identity and relationships decades later.

Why do some children overcome adversity so well while others do not? Another way to ask this is, what fosters resilience in children? I will first describe what is meant by resilience and adversity, and then I will explore key protective factors that can moderate the effects of hardship and thus contribute to resilience in children.

DEFINING RESILIENCE

Resilience is generally understood as a person's ability to function adequately following adversity. Psychologists describe resilience as the process of adapting well in the face of adversity, trauma, or significant sources of stress.[4] The *Handbook of Resilience in Children* offers a good definition of resilience as a "child's achievement of positive developmental outcomes and avoidance of maladaptive outcomes under adverse conditions."[5] In other words, if a child who has suffered significant hardship is later said to be managing the developmental tasks typical for their age and context well enough, the child is considered to be resilient.

---

[3]Ishmael Beah, *A Long Way Home: Memoirs of a Boy Soldier* (New York: Sarah Crichton Books, 2007).

[4]"Building Your Resilience," American Psychological Association, 2012, web.archive.org/web/20210119122454/https://www.apa.org/topics/resilience.

[5]Sam Goldstein and Robert B. Brooks, eds., *Handbook of Resilience in Children*, 2nd ed. (New York: Springer, 2013), 6.

Typical developmental tasks (or competencies) for children may include getting along with other children, listening to adults, doing well in school, and following the behavioral rules of their society in general.[6] Conversely, problematic development can be reflected in aggressive behaviors toward other children, social withdrawal, poor school performance, mental disorders such as depression, and violent or other antisocial behavior.

DESCRIBING ADVERSITY

Since the 1980s, resilience studies regularly reference Norman Garmezy's groundbreaking work, which defined resilience in terms of competence. His work also outlined a variety of acute as well as chronic adversities children face.[7] Building on Garmezy's work, resilience researchers sought ways to assess adversity in a child's life. To this end, they developed life event questionnaires that include physical (e.g., chronic illness, severe injury), family (e.g., divorce, parental death), and community (e.g., surviving a tornado, friend moving away) events.[8]

Another way to describe childhood adversity has emerged in the past twenty years from research conducted by the Centers for Disease Control and Prevention (CDC) and Kaiser Permanente beginning in 1995.[9] This

---

[6]Emily Crawford, Margaret O'Dougherty Wright, and Ann S. Masten, "Resilience and Spirituality in Youth," in *The Handbook of Spiritual Development in Childhood and Adolescence,* ed. Eugene C. Roehlkepartain, Pamela E. King, Linda M. Wagener, and Peter L. Benson (Thousand Oaks, CA: Sage, 2006), 356.

[7]For example, Norman Garmezy, "Vulnerability Research and the Issue of Primary Prevention," *American Journal of Orthopsychiatry* 41 (1971): 101-16; Norman Garmezy, "Stressors of Childhood," in *Stress, Coping, and Development in Children,* ed. Norman Garmezy and Michael Rutter (New York: McGraw-Hill, 1983); Norman Garmezy, "Stress-Resistant Children: The Search for Protective Factors," in *Recent Research in Developmental Psychopathology: Journal of Child Psychology and Psychiatry Book Supplement,* No. 4 (Oxford, UK: Pergamon Press, 1985); Norman Garmezy, Ann Masten, and Auke Tellegen, "The Study of Stress and Competence in Children: A Building Block for Developmental Psychopathology," *Child Development* 55 (1984): 97-111.

[8]See, for example, Scott D. Gest, Marie Gabrielle J. Reed, and Ann S. Masten, "Measuring Developmental Changes in Exposure to Adversity: A Life Chart and Rating Scale Approach," *Development and Psychopathology* 34 (1999): 509-26.

[9]"The Adverse Childhood Experiences (ACE) Study," Atlanta, GA: Centers for Disease Control and Prevention, National Center for Injury Prevention and Control, Division of Violence Prevention. May 2014. Archived from the original on 27 December 2015. Vincent J. Felitti et al., "Relationship of Childhood Abuse and Household Dysfunction to Many of the Leading Causes of Death in Adults: The Adverse Childhood Experiences (ACE) Study," *American Journal of Preventive Medicine* 14, no. 4 (1998); 245-58.

study was designed to assess social, emotional, and cognitive effects of experiences on children in three categories of adversity:

- Abuse: emotional, physical, or sexual abuse.
- Household challenges: child was treated violently by a parent; substance abuse or mental illness in the household; parents separated or divorced; incarcerated household member.
- Neglect: emotional or physical neglect.[10]

This research involved more than seventeen thousand participants who answered questions from a sixty-item family history questionnaire. Investigators found that adverse childhood experiences (ACEs) are common across all populations. Almost two-thirds of the participants reported at least one adverse child experience, and more than one in five reported three or more ACEs.

Criteria from Garmezy's work as well as the ACEs categories are considered appropriate ways of describing adversity or trauma. Researchers have also considered protective factors that can ameliorate the effects of adversity and trauma on children.

PROTECTIVE FACTORS THAT CAN ENCOURAGE RESILIENCE

Ann Masten has been contributing to resilience research for decades, having joined Garmezy in his work at the University of Minnesota in the 1970s. Her book *Ordinary Magic: Resilience in Development* condenses and integrates foundational and recent research on resilience in children and adolescents.[11] One study Masten examined was the Kauai Longitudinal Study of resilience, which followed 698 babies born in 1955 for several decades.[12] Around two hundred of the participants were

---

[10]"About the CDC-Kaiser ACE Study," Centers for Disease Control and Prevention, April 13, 2020, www.cdc.gov/violenceprevention/childabuseandneglect/acestudy/about.html.

[11]Ann Masten, *Ordinary Magic: Resilience in Development* (New York: Guilford Press, 2015).

[12]Masten, *Ordinary Magic*, 33-34; Masten cites Emmy E. Werner, "Risk, Resilience, and Recovery: Perspectives from the Kauai Longitudinal Study," *Development and Psychopathology* 5 (1993): 502-15; Emmy E. Werner and Ruth S. Smith, *Vulnerable but Invincible: A Study of Resilient Children* (New York: McGraw-Hill, 1982); Emmy E. Werner and Ruth S. Smith, *Overcoming the Odds: High Risk Children from Birth to Adulthood* (Ithaca, NY: Cornell University Press, 1992).

considered high-risk, a category that in this study included children living in situations of poverty, chronic family discord, parental mental or physical illness, or moderate to severe perinatal stress.[13] About two-thirds of the at-risk children developed significant problems between the ages of ten and eighteen (such as poor school performance, depression or anxiety, or substance abuse). Conversely, about a third of the participants appeared to be doing well: they were successful in school, socially competent, law-abiding, engaged in the community, and mentally healthy.[14]

As the researchers continued to follow both groups, they began to focus on factors that contributed to resilience in those who were doing well. They found that protective influences for these children included better quality caregiving from early childhood, more affirming and supportive relationships with parents and adults, more likable personalities, better cognitive skills, positive self-beliefs, and more faith and religious connections.[15]

Table 1. Protective factors and adaptive systems linked to resilience[16]

TEN PROTECTIVE FACTORS	BASIC HUMAN ADAPTIVE SYSTEMS
• Effective caregiving and parenting quality	• Attachment; family
• Close relationships with other capable adults	• Attachment; social networks
• Close friends and romantic partners (for youth)	• Attachment; peer and family systems
• Intelligence and problem-solving skills	• Learning and thinking systems of the central nervous system
• Self-control, emotional regulation, planfulness	• Self-regulation systems of the central nervous system
• Motivation to succeed	• Mastery motivation and reward systems
• Self-efficacy	• Mastery motivation
• Effective schools	• Education systems
• Effective neighborhoods, collective efficacy	• Functioning community systems
• Faith, hope, and the belief that life has meaning[17]	• Spiritual, religious, and cultural belief systems

---

[13]Masten, *Ordinary Magic*, 33.
[14]Masten, *Ordinary Magic*, 34.
[15]Masten, *Ordinary Magic*.
[16]Masten, *Ordinary Magic*, 148. Another source that categorizes various protective factors is Harvard University's "Supportive Relationships and Active Skill-Building Strengthen the Foundations of Resilience," National Scientific Council on the Developing Child, 2015, https://developing child.harvard.edu/resources/supportive-relationships-and-active-skill-building-strengthen -the-foundations-of-resilience/. This working paper addresses most of Masten's factors, but groups them somewhat differently.
[17]This factor has been moved to the last position in Masten's table.

Masten has drawn from the Kauai study as well as dozens of other resilience studies over the past several decades, sorting and organizing the findings and ultimately constructing a list of ten protective factors linked to resilience in young people, along with adaptive systems that can foster these resilience factors, as seen in table 1.

A brief explanation of these factors follows.

Capable parenting. If a child is in a difficult situation (e.g., fleeing war or living with type 1 diabetes), capable parenting can make a difference in the child's long-term resilience. Parents who listen to their children's fears and hopes, encourage their children, and carry the burden of the situation as adults contribute to the child's resilience.[18] Of course, sometimes the parents' ability to bear their responsibilities as parents can be compromised if they too are traumatized by the experience that is affecting their child (e.g., refugee status or death of another child in the family).

Close relationships. If the child has strong relationships with grandparents, parents of friends, or even peers, these relationships can promote resilience even if parents are unable to do so.

Intelligence. This protective factor does not mean children with higher IQs are necessarily more resilient; rather, the intelligence factor carries the idea that a working brain—one that is not compromised by injury or posttraumatic stress disorder or otherwise hampered in its ability to problem-solve—can contribute to resilience. One early definition of intelligence from David Weschler (a well-known researcher of intelligence in the twentieth century) fits well here: "the global capacity of the individual to act purposefully, to think rationally, and to deal effectively with the environment."[19]

Self-control, motivation to succeed, emotional regulation, self-efficacy. These are unique personal factors that often help children overcome difficulties. An eleven-year-old girl whose mother is in prison and whose father is dead declared in her first meeting with her mentor, "I'm going to go to Yale, and I am going to be a lawyer." This young girl sees a strong

---

[18]Chapter seven on parenting, children's spirituality, and resilience will more fully develop ways parents can support children in their spiritual development.

[19]As cited by Masten, *Ordinary Magic,* 154.

future for herself; she is already exhibiting an unusual level of self-efficacy and motivation to succeed, factors that can promote resilience.

Effective schools, effective neighborhoods, collective efficacy. These factors near the end of Masten's list are external factors. If a child and her family survive a fire that destroys their home, a well-functioning, responsible community can help her and her family recover from the trauma of the fire and begin the process of rebuilding. The child can go back to school; her family can go to the bank, their church, and the grocery store. Friends, neighbors, and extended family can surround this family with care and support, and the child can safely begin to recover. If, on the other hand, an entire community is destroyed, as was the case in the 2010 Haiti earthquake, children may not receive the support they need and may continue to feel vulnerable and frightened because the whole community is reeling from the same circumstances that are affecting the child.

Children coping with less public difficulties (e.g., family abuse, mental illness of a parent, poverty) benefit in general from effective schools and communities that introduce them to larger, more hopeful futures in which they may flourish. Though these children may struggle at home, well-trained and caring teachers, safe afterschool programs, good sports and music programs, and community recreational facilities provide healthy outlets that can encourage resilience.

SPIRITUALITY AS A PROTECTIVE FACTOR

Most relevant to our discussion is the last protective factor in Masten's list as listed above.

Faith, hope, and the belief that life has meaning. Shelly Melia, a licensed professional counselor specializing in grief and trauma, has recently categorized the protective factors developed by Masten and other resilience researchers into the following five groups:

- External resources (Masten's schools, communities, and cultural practices)
- Internal assets (Masten's self-efficacy, self-control, and motivation to succeed)

- Familial dynamics (Masten's parenting piece, along with extended family)
- Relationships/connectedness (Masten's "other close relationships")
- Faith/spirituality[20]

Of course, Melia's last category, faith/spirituality, connects directly with Masten's protective factor of faith, hope, and the belief that life has meaning.

Both spirituality and religion can promote resilience in children. Spirituality, as we have seen, is a quality present in all persons out of which they seek to establish relationship with self, others, and God (as they understand God). Religion, in contrast, is generally understood to be a cultural system of beliefs, understandings, and practices that connects humankind with the divine or the transcendent. Religion and spirituality are sometimes used interchangeably, though they are not synonymous. Nor are they mutually exclusive.

Religion can be quite spiritual, though it can exist without spirituality as institutions or doctrines. And conversely, some people view themselves as spiritual but not religious. In general, spirituality and religion intersect and frequently overlap.

Much research supports the idea that spirituality—including faith, hope, and religious belief—promotes resilience in children encountering adversity. For example, one study of resilience in children of incarcerated parents noted that church and faith were important to many of the children in the study.[21] One boy identified with Job, saying that even when Satan took things away from him, Job didn't curse God, and that God restored everything to Job; the boy then connected Job's struggles to his own feelings about his dad's imprisonment—the grief it had caused and even good things that had come from it. Another child in the study said that he prays: "I have to talk sometimes and I say a prayer and [my fear] just goes away."[22] The authors summarized their understanding of

---

[20]Shelly Melia, "The Role of Spirituality in Resilience" (paper presentation, Children's Spirituality Summit, Nashville, Tennessee, June 26, 2018).
[21]Ande Nesmith and Ebony Ruhland, "Children of Incarcerated Parents: Challenges and Resiliency, in Their Own Words," *Children and Youth Services Review* 30, no. 10 (2008): 1119-30.
[22]Nesmith and Ruhland, "Children of Incarcerated Parents," 1127.

the resilience-spirituality-religion interconnection in these children: "Church offered an immediate support group, while their faith helped them feel that their struggles had a deeper meaning."[23]

Resilience findings are connected to both religion and spirituality, and this book addresses both realms. Some chapters will focus more on how churches and believing families can lean into the spiritual practices of Christianity, while other chapters will concentrate more on holistic practices that can be used in any environment—including government, public school, and other secular settings.

Since resilience is connected to spirituality, those who work with children facing hardship will recognize that not only must the physical, emotional, and psychological needs of children be addressed, but their spiritual needs should be attended to as well. Nurturing their relationships with themselves, others, and God (as the child understands God) can be a profound part of the healing process for children who have survived trauma as well as for any child facing common troubles in life.

TWO POPULATIONS

We typically think of resilience primarily in regard to children who have faced extremely difficult situations, for example, those who have lived through the shock and loss of devastating population-wide traumas, those who have suffered personal injuries such as abuse or neglect, or those who have endured distresses such as parental divorce or chronic illness.

But many of us parent, teach, care for, or interact with children who have not yet been affected by extraordinary or even commonplace hardships; they have good-enough parents, neighborhoods, faith communities, schools, friends, and health. In fact, as noted earlier, children often live whole childhoods without encountering a natural disaster or the shattering grief and loss surrounding the death of a sibling or parent or their own serious illness.

Nevertheless, most children will experience roadblocks in one form or another on their way to adulthood, and one way to equip children to

---

[23]Nesmith and Ruhland, "Children of Incarcerated Parents," 1127.

face with resilience the difficulties they do encounter—large or small—is to help them establish foundational spiritual resources, especially their relationships with themselves, with others, and with God.

CONCLUSION

A growing body of research is linking religion and spirituality to resilience in children and adolescents.[24] Some studies indicate that religious involvement and spirituality are connected to self-esteem, social support, positive coping skills, and role identity, all qualities that engender resilience. Others found that having faith is related to hope and optimism—again, ways of being that contribute to perseverance. Religious and spiritual coping help children deal with stress and illness. In general, positive spiritual reframing of events can instill hope and meaning when a child is dealing with adversity.

Miguel, the child who witnessed the Sandy Hook shooting, is one such child. His father says Miguel does not often talk about the shooting, but he sometimes asks why it happened. His dad says the family tries to be honest, telling him they don't know why. When Miguel asks about his friends who were killed, his dad says, "We talk about heaven. He knows they're there."[25] This little boy is trying to make meaning, trying to understand, and his family is walking with him on this spiritual journey.

---

[24]See, e.g., Thema Bryant-Davis, Monica U. Ellis, Elizabeth Burke-Maynard, Nathan Moon, Pamela A. Counts, and Gera Anderson, "Religiosity, Spirituality, and Trauma Recovery in the Lives of Children and Adolescents," *Professional Psychology: Research and Practice* 43, no. 4 (2012): 306-14; Marie Good and Teena Willoughby, "Adolescence as a Sensitive Period for Spiritual Development," *Child Development Perspectives* 2 (2008): 32-37; Mark D. Holder, Ben Coleman, and Judi M. Wallace, "Spirituality, Religiousness, and Happiness in Children Aged 8-12 Years," *Journal of Happiness Studies* 11 (2010): 131-50.

[25]Associated Press, "'I Know Where the Bad Guy Is.'"

CHAPTER THREE

The Intersection of Children's Spirituality and Resilience

In July 2020, a YouTube video related to Covid-19 featured a four-year-old girl named Blake sitting at the kitchen table talking with her parents about life during the pandemic:

> Blake: "Everything in the whole world has to shut down; nobody can go anywhere 'cause they're shut down. The ice cream truck is shut down." (Blake starts to sob.) "The water park is shut down, which is my favorite place. And we can't go anywhere, not even McDonald's, which is my favorite restaurant. Everything in this town is shut all the way down. I don't want it to do that. And the only thing that is open . . . is nothing!"

> Blake's parents listen sympathetically, saying "Uh-huh," and "Yes, I know." Her mom lays her hand softly on Blake's arm.

> Blake continues: "I mean, why would germs come around people if they don't want germs to be around them? Because everyone doesn't like germs because they get sick, and everything has to be shut down 'cause people are sick, but everything that is fun also has to be shut down. And it's not fair."

> Mom: "I'm so sorry. It's a lot."

> Blake: "Yeah."

> Mom: "And it won't last forever."

> Blake: "Yeah, just for a few weeks."

> Dad: "And we're doing this so everyone can be safe, right?"

> Blake nods her head, then moves on to another subject.[1]

---

[1] "'The Ice Cream Truck Is Shut Down': 4-Year-Old Loses It over COVID-19 Lockdown," YouTube, July 13, 2020, www.youtube.com/watch?v=6GSLy-k0heI.

For some children, dealing with the restrictions of Covid-19 was the first significant difficulty they faced. Of course, not getting to swim at the water park isn't one of life's greatest hardships; nevertheless, this mildly humorous example offers a gentle opportunity to demonstrate how resilience and spirituality can be related.

Armed with our two basic descriptions of (1) children's spirituality as a quality present in every child out of which they seek to establish relationships with self, others, and God, and (2) resilience as a person's ability to function adequately following adversity, we will now look more closely at how these ideas intersect.

One key goal of resilience studies is to identify qualities that predict resilience in the face of adversity and ultimately to seek ways to promote these qualities—that is, to foster a "resilient mindset" in all children.[2] Among Masten's ten protective factors that we looked at in the last chapter are self-control, self-efficacy, and problem-solving skills. Other researchers include strong self-regulation skills, high self-esteem, and adequate prosocial skills in their lists of characteristics that lead to positive outcomes after loss, grief, or other hardship.[3] And as mentioned earlier, spirituality, religious commitment, and relationship with God also show up on various lists of factors that correlate with resilience.

Of course, none of these studies claims that any child who possesses, for example, good problem-solving skills or high self-esteem will simply float above adversity. Nor can we assert that nurturing children spiritually will protect them completely from negative outcomes when they suffer hardship. Nevertheless, it has been well documented that protective factors and particular qualities can have a moderating effect on children's outcomes after exposure to adverse experiences.[4]

---

[2]Sam Goldstein and Robert B. Brooks, "Why Study Resilience?" in *Handbook of Resilience in Children*, ed. Sam Goldstein and Robert B. Brooks, 2nd ed. (New York: Springer, 2013), 3.

[3]Nicole Racine et al., "Development of Trauma Symptoms Following Adversity in Childhood: The Moderating Role of Protective Factors," *Child Abuse & Neglect* 101 (March 2020): 104375.

[4]Goldstein and Brooks, *Handbook of Resilience in Children*; Ann Masten, *Ordinary Magic: Resilience in Development* (New York: Guilford Press, 2015); Tracie O. Afifi and Harriet L. Macmillan, "Resilience Following Child Maltreatment: A Review of Protective Factors," *Canadian Journal of Psychiatry* 56, no. 5 (2011): 266-72.

In addition to those already discussed, there are a number of other qualities, attitudes, and characteristics that researchers say buffer or moderate negative outcomes of adversity, and these factors also interconnect with spirituality. What are some of the other resilience qualities? I have developed the following list from resilience research:

- Trust
- Identity
- Problem-solving skills
- A sense of belonging
- Making meaning
- Purpose
- A sense of hope
- Gratitude
- Optimism
- Self-efficacy
- Self-awareness
- Self-regulation
- Motivation to succeed
- Receiving and giving social support
- Positive and supportive relationships with relatives, teachers, and other mentors[5]

Many of these resilience qualities correlate with the three relationships we are exploring: the child-self relationship, the child-others relationship, and the child-God relationship. Let's look at some of these qualities in more depth.

---

[5]Thema Bryant-Davis et al., "Religiosity, Spirituality, and Trauma Recovery in the Lives of Children and Adolescents," *Professional Psychology: Research and Practice* 43, no. 4 (2012): 306-14; Masten, *Ordinary Magic*; Leslie Roth and Trudelle Thomas, "Spirit Books: Promoting Conversation with Picture Books," *International Journal of Children's Spirituality* 18, no. 4 (2013): 351-68; Steven Sandage, Carol Aubrey, and Tammy Ohland, "Weaving the Fabric of Faith," *Marriage and Family: A Christian Journal* 2, no. 4 (1999): 381-98; David Crenshaw, "A Resilience Framework for Treating Severe Trauma," in *Handbook of Resilience in Children*, 309-27.

IDEПTITY

Children who are resilient tend to have a strong sense of identity.[6]

Elizabeth Smart was kidnapped when she was barely fourteen, shackled, raped repeatedly by her abductor, and kept captive for nine months. In her autobiography, she recalls words her mother had said to her some years before:

> Elizabeth, you're going to meet lots of people in this life. Some will like you. Some of them won't. But of all the people you'll have to deal with, there are only a few people that matter. God. And your dad and me. God will always love you. *You are His daughter.* He will never turn his back on you. The same thing is true for me. It doesn't matter where you go, or what you do, or whatever else might happen, I will always love you. *You will always be my daughter.* Nothing can change that.[7]

Smart writes that these words gave her hope as she endured the traumatic experiences of her captivity. Her identity as a child of God and as a beloved daughter in her family sustained her.

Much identity development literature focuses on adolescence and emerging adulthood as the years when people are keenly focused on who they are and who they are becoming. Though this is true, identity development doesn't begin in adolescence. Elizabeth at fourteen already knew at a foundational level that she was a child of God and a beloved daughter of her parents, understandings that she had integrated and absorbed into her very being in her childhood years before she was kidnapped. And those fundamental identities upheld her.

Hay and Nye (whose definition of children's spirituality we looked at in an earlier chapter) explain that the child-self and child-others relationships contribute to a child's growing sense of identity.[8] The conversation Elizabeth Smart had with her mother helped form her understanding of herself in relation to God and her family. Identity development even in younger children involves a cluster of questions like the following: *Who*

---

[6]Bryant-Davis et al., "Religiosity, Spirituality, and Trauma Recovery."
[7]Elizabeth Smart with Chris Stewart, *My Story* (New York: St. Martin's Griffin, 2014), 60. Emphasis added.
[8]David Hay with Rebecca Nye, *The Spirit of the Child,* rev. ed. (London: Jessica Kingsley, 2006).

am I? Who am I called to become? Why am I here? What will I be when I grow up? When children engage with these questions thoughtfully, they are more likely to grow in resilience, perseverance, and confidence.[9]

TRUST AND HOPE

Early patterns of trust are crucial for a baby's healthy emotional and social development. After they come into the world, infants are asking, *Can I trust the people around me?* Erik Erikson considers navigating the trust-versus-mistrust task to be the most basic psychosocial crisis for children, and he connects trust development directly to hope.[10] For example, if a two-year-old enters the next developmental stage (autonomy versus shame and doubt) with more trust than mistrust, the child carries the virtue of hope forward. Generally, if parents and caregivers are consistent in providing food, warmth, comfort, and affection, infants learn trust. Trust, however, can be compromised in later stages of life.

Children who have been neglected or abused find it very difficult to trust. One task of counselors, social workers, foster parents, and others who work with children who have been maltreated is to help them renegotiate that trust-versus-mistrust crisis successfully, since learning to trust is part of the process of recovery. It is also a key factor in resilience. When life falls apart and nothing seems stable, learning to trust again is a crucial step in being willing to move into a new future—that is, to hope.

After forty-two years of direct clinical work with severely traumatized children, David Crenshaw says hope is the cornerstone of successful therapy.[11] Children who have suffered multiple traumas or chronic long-term abuse find it very difficult to begin to hope, since hope has been crushed so many times in the past. For these children to live into a better future, they must begin to believe the possibility that there *is* a good

---

[9]Roth and Thomas, "Spirit Books."

[10]Erik Erikson developed eight stages of healthy psychosocial development. In each stage the child or adult is navigating a psychological crisis (e.g., trust versus mistrust), which, if navigated successfully, yields a "psychosocial strength" or virtue. Erik Erikson, *Childhood and Society,* 2nd ed. (New York: Norton, 1963).

[11]David Crenshaw, "A Resilience Framework for Treating Severe Trauma," in *Handbook of Resilience in Children,* ed. Goldstein and Brooks, (New York: Springer Science+Business Media, 2013), 309-27.

future—and that is hope. In Crenshaw's opinion, resilience cannot function without hope.

Of course, both hope and trust are spiritual qualities. Jesuit author Joseph Appleyard writes that spiritual development is about one's relationship with God, "partly about knowing, but also about trusting and being acknowledged by whom one trusts."[12] Masten includes hope as part of the protective factor she describes as faith, hope, and the belief that life has meaning.[13] Bryant-Davis and colleagues say possessing a sense of hope is a spiritual coping strategy.[14] And the psalmist connects these two spiritual concepts: "May your unfailing love be with us, LORD, even as we put our hope in you" (Psalm 33:22). The writer of Hebrews makes the same connection: "Let us hold unswervingly to the hope we profess, for he who promised is faithful" (Hebrews 10:23). These are verses that can carry a child waiting in the dark for morning to come; they give assurance—they remind a child that God is here and is at work.

A SENSE OF BELONGING

"Belongingness" is the third tier in Maslow's hierarchy of needs.[15] After their physical needs and safety needs are met, human beings seek—and need—places to belong. Children especially need to feel a deep sense of belonging. Healthy belongingness offers support for children in difficult situations. Not surprisingly, having a strong sense of belonging is a quality that contributes to resilience.[16]

A sense of belonging is particularly important in the realm of spiritual care and formation.[17] "Being wanted, welcomed, invited, and included are some of the most mending experiences on the planet," according to one spiritual formation leader.[18] Realizing they have a place where people

---

[12]J. A. Appleyard, "Imagination's Arc: The Spiritual Development of Readers," in *Seeing into the Life of Things*, ed. John L. Mahoney (New York: Fordham University Press, 1998), 56.

[13]Masten, *Ordinary Magic*.

[14]Bryant-Davis et al., "Religiosity, Spirituality, and Trauma Recovery."

[15]Abraham Maslow, *Motivation and Personality* (New York: Harper & Brothers, 1954).

[16]Bryant-Davis et al., "Religiosity, Spirituality, and Trauma Recovery."

[17]Steven Sandage, Carol Aubrey, and Tammy Ohland, "Weaving the Fabric of Faith," *Marriage and Family: A Christian Journal* 2, no. 4 (1999): 381-98.

[18]Adele Ahlberg Calhoun, *Invitations from God: Accepting God's Offer to Rest, Weep, Forgive, Wait, Remember, and More* (Downers Grove, IL: InterVarsity Press), 10.

know them and love them, receive them and care for them, can fortify children in even the most extreme circumstances. And when children suffer population-wide disasters, finding a new place to belong is a key component of their emotional, psychological, and spiritual recovery.

MAKING MEANING

As mentioned at the end of the last chapter, constructing meaning around adversity seems to contribute to resilience in children. Masten says the belief that life has meaning is a protective factor in children's lives and that out of this belief children like Miguel ask questions such as, "Why did this happen?"

Many researchers connect the process of making meaning to spirituality. Bryant-Davis and her colleagues say making meaning is a spiritual coping strategy (along with a sense of belonging and a sense of hope).[19] Robert Coles, the well-known child psychiatrist and author, says that children call on their spiritual values to understand why things have happened to them.[20] Others see spirituality as the developmental engine that propels the search for meaning and purpose.[21] Creating opportunities for children to safely ask their "why" questions is important to their ability to move beyond their present fear.

SELF-REGULATION, SELF-MOTIVATION, SELF-EFFICACY, AGENCY

Individual characteristics that often lead to positive outcomes in the face of adversity include good self-regulation skills, self-motivation, self-efficacy, and a sense of agency:[22]

- Self-regulation: the ability to manage one's emotions and actions appropriately.

---

[19]Bryant-Davis et al., "Religiosity, Spirituality, and Trauma Recovery."
[20]Robert Coles, *The Spiritual Life of Children* (Boston: Houghton Mifflin, 1990), 100.
[21]Eugene C. Roehlkepartain, Pamela E. King, Linda M. Wagener, and Peter L. Benson, "The Spiritual Development in Childhood and Adolescence," in *Handbook of Spiritual Development in Childhood and Adolescence*, ed. Peter Benson, Eugene Roehlkepartain, Pamela King, and Linda Wagener (London: Sage Publications, 2005), 5-6.
[22]Masten, *Ordinary Magic*; Racine et al., "Development of Trauma Symptoms."

- Self-motivation: the ability to motivate oneself to start or continue a task without being prodded by someone else.
- Self-efficacy: the belief that one can succeed in specific situations or accomplish a task.
- A sense of agency: the ability to make choices and decisions that influence events and have an impact on one's world.

Each of these traits has been linked to resilience. That is, children who can recognize and articulate their feelings, regulate their responses to certain emotions, and advocate for what they need are often more able to succeed in a context of severe adversity.[23]

At first glance, these "personal" resilience qualities could be seen as residing in the individual as hereditary strengths or qualities of temperament. And indeed, this may be so to a degree. For example, some children seem to arrive in this world with a strong voice advocating for their own needs while others seem generally content to receive whatever is given.

Even though some of these individual characteristics seem to be innate or gene-related, all of them can be fostered through conversations where feelings, preferences, needs, desires, and appropriate behavior are discussed in a warm, loving environment. They are not all-or-nothing qualities. And all children can learn to better regulate their emotions and actions and grow in self-motivation and self-efficacy. Children can gain a sense of agency while interacting with encouraging parents, teachers, and caregivers.

We recently visited our twenty-two-month-old grandson (and his parents), and I was privileged to tuck him in bed each night. I would choose several books to read, then hold up two at a time and ask Roham which he would like for me to read. He delighted in quickly choosing one. After reading that book, I would hold up two more and he would choose. Roham was experiencing agency—that is, he was influencing the events around him. He was doing this at a very minimal level, of

---

[23]Masten, *Ordinary Magic*; also, "Supportive Relationships and Active Skill-Building Strengthen the Foundations of Resilience," National Scientific Council on the Developing Child, Center on the Developing Child at Harvard University, 2015, https://developingchild.harvard.edu/resources /supportive-relationships-and-active-skill-building-strengthen-the-foundations-of-resilience/.

course, but nevertheless he was given the opportunity to choose and he did so. Being encouraged to choose fosters a sense of agency, even in one this young.

This illustration also is an example of the child-others relationship that is so crucial in developing qualities related to resilience. In fact, the significance of healthy relationships is an item on virtually every list of resilience factors. For example:

- Three items on Masten's list of resilience factors focus on relationships: effective caregiving and parenting quality, close relationships with other capable adults, and close friends and romantic partners (for youth).[24]

- Goldstein and Brooks say children with a resilient mindset will be able to relate comfortably with others.[25]

- Judith Jordan with Harvard Medical School says that relationships are at *the heart* of growth and resilience.[26]

- Resnick and his colleagues say the single best predictor of resilience is having a good relationship with one adult, such as a teacher, parent, or mentor.[27]

POSITIVE AND SUPPORTIVE RELATIONSHIPS WITH RELATIVES, TEACHERS, AND OTHER MENTORS

As just indicated, strong and healthy relationships between children and others are a vital component of resilience. These relationships profoundly affect all other resilience qualities and protective factors. Just considering the characteristics briefly outlined above, it is clear that trust is built within relationships. A sense of belonging cannot happen alone—if it exists, there must be others involved. Identity is hammered out within

---

[24]Masten, *Ordinary Magic,* 148.

[25]Goldstein and Brooks, "Why Study Resilience?," 3.

[26]Judith V. Jordan, "Relational Resilience in Girls," in *Handbook of Resilience in Children,* ed. Sam Goldstein and Robert B. Brooks, 2nd ed. (New York: Springer, 2013).

[27]Michael Resnick, Kathleen Harris, and Robert Blum, "The Impact of Caring and Connectedness on Adolescent Health and Well-Being," *Journal of Pediatrics and Child Health* 29, no. 1, (1993): S3-S9; also Harvard University's "Supportive Relationships and Active Skill-Building Strengthen the Foundations of Resilience."

families, in churches, in communities, within ethnicities—with other people. It is difficult for a child to make sense of life events (making meaning) without others around to respond to questions, and even those "self-" qualities described in the preceding section are best developed with guidance, modeling, and encouragement from others. Thus, just as the child-others piece of the children's spirituality definition is essential for spiritual development, it is also—not surprisingly—indispensable for resilience as well. Most studies that indicate that social support from others is important for the development of resilience have emphasized *one-way* support, that is, *getting* love and *getting* help. However, Jordan encourages the notion that ultimately social support can and should be about *mutuality* not just about receiving.[28] In other words, part of the journey toward wholeness—and resilience—can be *giving* help and *giving* support to others. For example, Elizabeth Smart in the ensuing years after her rescue began to work as an activist and advocate for missing persons.

CONCLUSION

In the YouTube video in which Blake complains about everything fun being shut down, we notice several ways her parents are helping build resilience in their daughter.

Agency. First, they allow Blake to express her dismay over the losses she is experiencing. While they (and we) know that not getting to buy ice cream or visit the water park are small deprivations, to a four-year-old they feel large, especially when experienced cumulatively. By taking her complaints seriously and giving her a legitimate voice, Blake's parents are contributing to their daughter's sense of agency. Mom and Dad listen respectfully, demonstrating to Blake that her perspective and her feelings matter. They could have shut down the complaints immediately, saying, for example, "Blake, there are people dying out there; giving up the water park is nothing. That's enough of that whining." Nor did her parents take her frustrations *too* seriously; they didn't immediately hop up and find a place to buy Blake some

---

[28]Jordan, "Relational Resilience."

ice cream or promise her a trip to the lake since they couldn't go to the water park. They listened and commiserated with her losses.

Hope. Blake is catastrophizing the present situation when she says, "Everything is shut down. The only thing that's open . . . is nothing."

Her parents could have simply said, "That's not true, Blake," and begun naming places that were open. But they leaned into her comments, saying church was also closed, generally agreeing that their lives had really changed. And then the mom says, "It won't last forever."

At this point Blake begins to convey a quieter spirit, and we see her move away from the tears and overstatements. This approach acknowledges the present realities but also assures the child that these realities will not always be so; the current situation will change.

Making meaning. Blake herself attempts to explain the pandemic and the resulting negative consequences when she says, "Why would germs come around people if they don't want germs to be around them? Because everyone doesn't like germs because they get sick, and everything has to be shut down 'cause people are sick, but everything that is fun also has to be shut down. And it's not fair."

Her attempts are not completely logical, but her parents do not denigrate her thoughts. And later the dad helps clarify the "why" question when he says, "And we're doing this so everyone can be safe, right?"

Relationships. The child-others relationship is being deeply nurtured in this conversation. Blake's parents demonstrate that her feelings matter; they listen, and Blake trusts them to hear her. The child-self relationship has also clearly been nurtured; Blake is able to name her feelings. At one point she says, "It's just so frustrating"—rather advanced vocabulary for a four-year-old. She recognizes her feeling of frustration, and because her parents (or others) have helped her understand and name that feeling, she can communicate well that this is what she is feeling.

In summary, Blake's parents are modeling a variety of resilience-building behaviors and attitudes for their daughter. These kinds of conversations build trust and hope, they provide opportunities for making meaning together, and they nurture relationships. These are spiritual conversations, and spiritual conversations build resilience.

If this conversation between Blake and her parents seems ordinary, if it doesn't seem profoundly spiritual, then this illustration has done what I hoped it would do. One of my goals is to help parents, teachers, counselors, social workers, and children's ministers see that nurturing children spiritually is less complicated and formal than we perhaps have imagined. Building resilience in children can be a natural part of ordinary conversations.

In other words, building a resilient mindset is what we do when we provide children with opportunities to develop the skills, qualities, and characteristics necessary to fare well in the face of adversity that may or may not lie ahead.[29]

Though children have an inborn spirituality that is their greatest source of resilience,[30] they need adults to come around them and support that inherent spiritual quality. The following chapters will focus on ways adults can nurture children spiritually in order to assist them in becoming resilient as they cope with current circumstances and to prepare them for the unavoidable hardships of childhood.

---

[29]Goldstein and Brooks, "Why Study Resilience?"
[30]Miller, *The Spiritual Child.*

PART TWO

Families, Children's Spirituality, and Resilience

CHAPTER FOUR

Parenting, Children's Spirituality, and Resilience

Haileﬀ, a ﬀoung mother, anxiously said to me recently, "I know I should start devotionals with my baby. When should I start reading the Bible to him? I feel like I am already behind." She looked at me with a pinched, worried face.

I asked her how old her baby was, and she replied, "Four months. But I know I should already be doing something!"

I asked her, "Do you hold your baby?"

She said, "Yes, of course."

"Do you feed your baby?"

"Well, of course."

"Do you soothe your baby when he frets?"

"I try to."

With joy I responded, "Hailey, you are nurturing your baby spiritually. All of these wonderful things tell your baby he is loved, cherished, and cared for."

Lisa Miller agrees with me when she says, "Strong and healthy parental love can fill much of the spiritual developmental need."[1]

Some parts of this chapter were published previously as Holly C. Allen with Christa Adams, Kara Jenkins, and Jill Meek, "How Parents Nurture the Spiritual Development of Their Children: Insights from Recent Qualitative Research," in *Understanding Children's Spirituality: Theology, Research, and Practice,* ed. Kevin Lawson (Eugene, OR: Cascade, 2012), 197-222. Used by permission of Wipf and Stock Publishers, www.wipfandstock.com.

[1]Lisa Miller, *The Spiritual Child: The New Science on Parenting for Health and Lifelong Thriving* (New York: St. Martin's Press, 2015), 100.

During those first few months and years of life, parental care and love are the crucial ingredients that build directly on the child's already existing spirituality.[2] Of course, as the months and years go by, there are additional ways parents can nurture their children's spiritual formation, though love will continue to be the foundational spiritual language.

In recent decades Western culture has not in general been welcoming to children's spirituality. In fact, most children, though they may exhibit a strong sense of spirituality in the preschool years, by the age of eight or ten recognize that speaking about spiritual matters is socially unacceptable on the whole.[3] Children and youth get little support from schools, media, or culture to develop their inherent spiritual essence.[4] They need support from parents and a faith community to flourish spiritually. Without it, their inborn spirituality may begin to wane.

However, many parents hesitate. Some want their children to develop spiritually on their own. Some think the church should take care of their children's spiritual life. Others may want to nurture their children spiritually but simply do not know how.[5]

Spiritual strength is a key factor in resilience in children (and adults). Beyond the critically necessary unconditional love and care mentioned previously, how can parents foster a spirituality in their children that will sustain them when hardships come?

BEST PRACTICES

Four core themes appear repeatedly in literature and research that can serve as recommendations to parents who seek to nurture their children's religious and spiritual development: (1) foster religious or spiritual conversation and discussion, (2) participate with children in religious

---

[2]See chapter one for a fuller explanation of the idea that children are spiritual beings from birth.
[3]Miller, *The Spiritual Child*, 1-22.
[4]However, in November 2019, Teachers College of Columbia University in New York hosted a conference called "The Next Wave in K-12 Education: The Spiritual Core of the Whole Child," which explored the idea of spirituality as the next frontier in the field of education. I am encouraged that spirituality as a construct could be reintroduced in public schools. Though the Columbia conference's definition of spirituality would not necessarily include God, acknowledging human beings as spiritual beings is a start.
[5]For a fuller exploration of some parents' hesitation to influence their children's spirituality, see Miller, *The Spiritual Child*, 10-11.

activities or rituals, (3) model a congruent spiritual life before children, and (4) parent lovingly yet firmly. As we look at each of these practices in depth, we will note how they interconnect with the three relational aspects of children's spirituality that frame most of the discussions of this book: the child-God relationship, the child-others relationship, and the child-self relationship.

Ordinary conversation: talk about it. Lacy Finn Borgo's lyrical book *Spiritual Conversations with Children* explores how spiritual conversations with children support their life with God.[6] When I read Borgo's book, she had me from the moment she used the phrase "one-with-one listening"—rather than "one-on-one." This small adjustment captures the essence of Borgo's beautiful book as she shows us how to come alongside children on their spiritual journey.

Though Borgo has written her book for those who desire to be spiritual directors with children, her insights are keenly relevant for parents: "In spiritual conversations with children, the listening adult makes room for the child to recognize God's presence and respond to this recognition."[7]

Borgo offers several questions to use with children who come for spiritual direction, but they of course are also excellent questions for parents to ask their children:

- Will you tell me about a time when you and God did something together?
- Will you tell me a story about something good that happened to you?
- Will you tell me a story of a very strong emotion you had this week? It could be happiness or sadness or anger—anything.
- Will you tell me the story of the most beautiful thing you have ever seen?
- Will you tell me the story of a time when you felt safe or scared?
- Is there something you would like to talk about? I am here to listen.[8]

---

[6]Lacy Finn Borgo, *Spiritual Conversations with Children: Listening to God Together* (Downers Grove, IL: InterVarsity Press, 2020), 3.
[7]Borgo, *Spiritual Conversations,* 41.
[8]Borgo, *Spiritual Conversations,* 71-72.

The discussions that emerge through these prompts can nurture all three relationships: the child-self, child-others, and child-God relationship.

Though people tend to associate spirituality with a sense of other-worldliness—and indeed transcendent experiences certainly can nurture faith and foster a relationship with God—commonplace, prosaic experiences also foster spirituality. Running errands, driving to the next activity, completing chores and household projects together, and eating meals as a family all provide opportunities for ordinary discussion and insight that cultivate those relationships.

Chris Boyatzis shares the delightful story of his three-year-old at bath time talking about "bath-tizing" the soap.[9] While his daughter bath-tized (and re-bath-tized) the soap, Boyatzis described for her the events surrounding her own baptism when she was an infant, and that initial discussion led to subsequent conversations over the years regarding her baptism.

Brad Wigger encourages parents to reflect on daily situations and theological questions alike with their children.[10] These reflections enable spiritual development for both parents and children, as children often have insights that are helpful and challenging for adults. Children are very inquisitive; they want to know more about God. They want to know what their parents think and believe; they listen. Certainly, Scripture offers clear understanding that ordinary but frequent parent-child conversation is a key means of fostering children's spiritual growth and development:

> Hear, O Israel: The LORD our God, the LORD is one. Love the LORD your God with all your heart and with all your soul and with all your strength. These commandments that I give you today are to be on your hearts. Impress them on your children. Talk about them when you sit at home and when you walk along the road, when you lie down and when you get up. Tie them as symbols on your hands and bind them on your

---

[9]Chris Boyatzis, "The Co-Construction of Spiritual Meaning in Parent-Child Communication," in *Children's Spirituality: Christian Perspectives, Research, and Applications*, ed. Don Ratcliff (Eugene, OR: Cascade, 2004), 183.

[10]Brad J. Wigger, *The Power of God at Home: Nurturing Our Children in Love and Grace* (San Francisco: Jossey-Bass Books, 2003).

foreheads. Write them on the doorframes of your houses and on your gates. (Deuteronomy 6:4-9)

The children in my dissertation interviews were quick to offer examples of regular conversational engagement with their parents about everyday events and spiritual matters.[11] When Boaz (age eleven) became interested in reading the Harry Potter books, he discussed the idea with his dad. Boaz noted, "My dad is reading the first Harry Potter book to see if it's okay." Cornelius (age ten) mentioned in his interview that he also discussed the Harry Potter books with his mom, and they made a decision regarding the books after they had both prayed about the matter. These parents took the time to discuss everyday decisions with their children, and the children remembered those conversations and told them to me in response to the question, "What is it about your [parent] makes you think they know God?"

When I asked Joanna (age eleven) what she would do if she wanted to get to know God, she said, "I would probably ask my parents [about] things I don't know about him and I would tell them the things I do know about him and they could tell me." Lydia (also eleven), in response to the question, "Of all the people you know, who do you think knows God the best?" replied, "Mom, because of the way that she tells me about God, the way she talks about God, how she respects him." Both Joanna's and Lydia's comments indicate that frequent easy conversations about God characterize their homes.

Family religious activities or rituals: do it. The resilience and spirituality literature indicates that part of the spirituality factor can be overt religious experience.[12] Many children have these experiences with their

---

[11]The interviews were part of the field research for my dissertation: Holly J. Allen, "A Qualitative Study Exploring the Similarities and Differences of the Spirituality of Children in Intergenerational and Non-Intergenerational Christian Contexts" (PhD diss., Biola University, 2002). In 2009, Christa Adams, Kara Blood Jenkins, and Jill Williams Meek, students at John Brown University where I was teaching at the time, analyzed and coded the 250 pages of raw data collected from these interviews, focusing particularly on what children said about their parents. Since the original purpose of the dissertation had not focused on parents per se, the raw data had not been fully analyzed in light of children's comments about their parents.

[12]See, for example, Emily Crawford, Margaret O'Dougherty Wright, and Ann S. Masten, "Resilience and Spirituality in Youth," in *The Handbook of Spiritual Development in Childhood and Adolescence*, ed. Eugene C. Roehlkepartain, Pamela E. King, Linda M. Wagener, and Peter L. Benson (Thousand Oaks, CA: Sage, 2006).

families. Some families light a candle when Scripture is read, make special foods for certain religious celebrations, say prayers before meals, or decorate their homes for Christmas or Easter.[13] "Rituals are embodied ways of celebrating God's presence in the midst of ordinary life. They take the common stuff of life and reveal its sacramental capacity," says spiritual formation specialist Marjorie Thompson.[14]

An early assignment in the course I teach on children's spirituality requires students to write a five-page reflection paper describing significant childhood spiritual influences. Typically, about half of the students describe in loving detail the nightly routines of Bible story reading and prayer their mothers and fathers led them in. Here is an example from one of my students: "My mom and dad . . . always came in to tuck me in and say our nightly prayers when I was young. It was my favorite time because it brought me closer and closer to my parents. We would talk about prayer and why we pray to God." Though these bedtime routines seem mundane (and sometimes interminable) to parents, the reflections of these students testify to the abiding effect such ordinary rituals can have.

In my research interviews, many of the children described these same bedtime routines.[15] Sara (age eleven) shared how her parents "always come in to pray with me at night before I go to bed; my dad normally comes in first. They keep telling me and my sisters how much they love us." Seth (age ten) said, "I pray every night with my mom before I go to bed." Priscilla (age eleven) said, "Each night my mom comes into each of our rooms and prays about things with us and she prays about times when we are having trouble."

One last vital family practice recommended by experts,[16] reported in retrospective studies,[17] and noted by faithful teens and emerging

---

[13]Marjorie J. Thompson, *Family: The Forming Center* (Nashville: Upper Room Books, 1996).

[14]Thompson, *Family*, 88.

[15]Allen, interviews conducted for "A Qualitative Study."

[16]Ivy Beckwith, *Postmodern Children's Ministry: Ministry to Children in the 21st Century* (Grand Rapids, MI: Zondervan, 2004); Catherine Stonehouse, *Joining Children on the Spiritual Journey: Nurturing a Life of Faith* (Grand Rapids, MI: Baker Books, 1998); John Westerhoff III, *Will Our Children Have Faith*, rev. ed. (Toronto: Morehouse, 2000).

[17]Marcia McQuitty, "A Qualitative Understanding of Deuteronomy 6," in *Nurturing Children's Spirituality: Christian Perspectives and Best Practices*, ed. Holly C. Allen (Eugene, OR: Cascade,

adults[18] is the importance of regularly attending worship services as a family—that is, going to church. As ordinary and familiar as it seems, going to church as a family is mentioned repeatedly by teens and adults who have maintained their Christian faith as a family ritual that critically informed and shaped their spiritual journeys.

Modeling: be who you say you are. In ordinary language, one might call this practicing what you preach. And in fact, in a study exploring sacred practices of highly religious families, a major theme that emerged was "practicing [and parenting] what you preach."[19] One of the participants in the study, a father of three, said:

> It's not what you do in the [church] building; it's what you do outside the building. When everyday life struggles challenge you, are you able to overcome adversity, are you able to withstand the things that are being thrown at you? Are you living the walk of faith or are you living like the world's living? Are you practicing what you preach?[20]

Other parents in the study repeatedly described the importance of living before their children the key tenets of their religion.

Later studies of highly religious families identified other processes that reflect the importance of parents modeling a congruent spirituality before their children.[21] These processes include "living religion at home," "loving and serving others in the family," and "abstaining from proscribed activities and substances."[22]

The children in my research named a plethora of qualities people who know God display. They said people who know God are kind (or nice),

---

2008); Robert Wuthnow, *Growing Up Religious: Christians and Jews and Their Religious Journeys of Faith* (Boston: Beacon, 1999).

[18]Christian Smith with Melinda Denton, *Soul Searching: The Religious and Spiritual Lives of American Teenagers* (New York: Oxford University Press, 2005); Christian Smith with Patricia Snell, *Souls in Transition: The Religious and Spiritual Lives of Emerging Adults* (New York: Oxford University Press, 2009).

[19]Loren D. Marks, "Sacred Practices in Highly Religious Families: Christian, Jewish, Mormon, and Muslim Perspectives," *Family Processes* 43 (2004): 217-31.

[20]Marks, "Sacred Practices," 222.

[21]David C. Dollahite and Loren D. Marks, "How Highly Religious Families Strive to Fulfill Sacred Purposes," in *Sourcebook of Family Theory and Research*, ed. Vern L. Bengston et al. (Thousand Oaks, CA: Sage, 2005); David C. Dollahite and Loren D. Marks, "A Conceptual Model of Family and Religious Processes in Highly Religious Families," *Review of Religious Research* 50, no. 4 (2009): 373-91.

[22]Dollahite and Marks, "How Highly Religious Families," 534-36.

calm, generous, patient, faithful, committed, disciplined, and loving. They do what is right, help people, and obey God. Several children offered a global description of character in general by saying that people who know God simply "act like it."[23]

Among those who said a parent was one of the adults in their lives who knew God well, twelve children mentioned some aspect of their mother's character and thirteen mentioned their father's character as evidence that they knew God. Noah commented about his dad, "Well, he's always kind of calm when there's strife going through the house." Nathaniel added, "He [Dad] is very faithful to do what he says. He has made mistakes, like he has forgotten his promise and not done it, but that happens sometimes. He always tries."[24]

Additionally, the children interviewed were clearly aware of their parents' spiritual practices. Children said they believed their parents knew God because of the amount of time they spent with God and the joy they demonstrated in worship. Sara recounted: "[My mom] spends a lot of time with [God]. She just had the last month off and she went to Sacramento. She spent the night there. She brought her notes, and her journal, and her music. She just will sit in her room sometimes and worship and write." Tabitha said of her father, "I see him praying a lot actually and having quiet times with God." And another child, Hannah, recalled the way her father worshiped God through dance.[25]

Altogether, fifteen out of the thirty-four children who mentioned parents believed that their parents knew God because they read the Bible every day, ten connected their parents' prayer life with knowing God, thirteen connected their parents' involvement in ministry or Bible studies to their knowledge of God, fourteen mentioned a characteristic or personality trait in their parents that signified knowing God, and ten said their parents knew God because they went to church every Sunday. The children had observed and were very aware of their parents' character and their spiritual lives.

---

[23]Allen, interviews conducted for "A Qualitative Study."
[24]Allen, interviews conducted for "A Qualitative Study."
[25]Allen, interviews conducted for "A Qualitative Study."

Children need to see their parents setting time aside for prayer, worship, reflection, and open discussion about issues of faith. According to Ivy Beckwith:

> If the child's parents and caregivers show that listening to and following God's story is a priority for them, then the child will model those attitudes. If the important adults in the child's life practice the spiritual disciplines, worship God, and make time to care for their own souls, then the child will find ways to mirror these behaviors in her own life.[26]

Sadly, other researchers have found the flip side of this truth to be true as well. When children see parents not "practicing what they preach," it can affect their spirituality negatively. David Kinnaman's massive studies (with the Barna Group) over many years reveal that one of the key reasons emerging adults leave their faith is the hypocrisy they see in parents or other adults; these perceptive young people crave authenticity.[27] Children see and take in the spiritual examples of their parents for good or for ill. Tabitha said of her mother, "When I see her worshiping, she is not worried about everybody else around her. She really connects with God and she closes her eyes and really does not have a lot of social interactions with everyone else while we are supposed to be worshiping and I look to that as an example."[28]

Responsive yet firm parenting: capable parenting. One of the ten factors Masten describes in her seminal work on resilience is capable parenting.[29] First, let's look at a widely used typology of parenting styles developed by Diana Baumrind in the 1960s and 1970s. Baumrind outlined three parenting styles, which she called authoritarian, authoritative, and permissive,[30] and later other psychologists added a fourth, the

---

[26]Beckwith, *Postmodern Children's Ministry*, 53.

[27]David Kinnaman, *You Lost Me: Why Young Christians Are Leaving Church . . . and Rethinking Faith* (Grand Rapids, MI: Baker, 2011); George Barna and David Kinnaman, *Churchless: Understanding Today's Unchurched and How to Connect with Them* (Grand Rapids, MI: Baker, 2014).

[28]Allen, interviews conducted for "A Qualitative Study."

[29]Ann Masten, *Ordinary Magic: Resilience in Development* (New York: Guilford Press, 2015).

[30]Diana Baumrind, "Effects of Authoritative Parental Control on Child Behavior," *Child Development* 37 (1966): 887-907; Diana Baumrind, "Parental Disciplinary Patterns and Social Competence in Children," *Youth and Society* 9 (1978): 239-76; Diana Baumrind, "The Influence of Parenting Style on Adolescent Competence and Substance Use," *Journal of Early Adolescence* 11 (1991): 56-95; Diana Baumrind, "The Discipline Controversy Revisited," *Family Relations* 45 (1996): 405-14.

neglecting-indifferent (or uninvolved) style.[31] Baumrind describes these parenting styles along two dimensions: responsiveness and directiveness (or control).[32]

The first dimension, responsiveness, is the degree to which parents respond to their children and provide affection. In table 2, this dimension forms the horizontal axis—responsiveness, affection, and support. The second dimension, the vertical axis, involves the degree of control parents employ with children. Table 2 reveals Baumrind's four parenting styles resulting from these two interfacing dimensions: authoritarian, authoritative, permissive, and neglectful.

Table 2. Baumrind's four parenting styles[33]

DIRECTIVE/CONTROLLING	RESPONSIVE/SUPPORTIVE: HIGH	RESPONSIVE/SUPPORTIVE: LOW
HIGH	**AUTHORITATIVE** • Responsive, supportive • Exhibit control	**AUTHORITARIAN** • Unsupportive • Demanding, controlling
LOW	**PERMISSIVE/INDULGENT** • Responsive, supportive • Indulgent, nondemanding	**NEGLECTFUL/INDIFFERENT** • Disengaged, uninvolved • Little discipline

[31]Eleanor E. Maccoby and J. A. Martin, "Socialization in the Context of the Family: Parent-Child Interaction," in Paul H. Mussen and E. Mavis Hetherington, eds., *Manual of Child Psychology*, vol. 4: Social Development (New York: John Wiley and Sons, 1983), 1-101.

[32]Baumrind, "The Influence of Parenting."

[33]Adapted from the work of Diana Baumrind: "Effects of Authoritative Parental Control on Child Behavior," *Child Development* 37 (1966): 887-907; "Parental Disciplinary Patterns and Social Competence in Children," *Youth and Society* 9 (1978): 239-76; "The Influence of Parenting Style on Adolescent Competence and Substance Use," *Journal of Early Adolescence* 11 (1991): 56-95; and "The Discipline Controversy Revisited," *Family Relations* 45 (1996): 405-14. Also Eleanor E. Maccoby and J. A. Martin, "Socialization in the Context of the Family: Parent-Child Interaction," in Mussen and Hetherington, *Manual of Child Psychology*, 1–101.

Extremely authoritarian parents (upper right-hand quadrant) tend to be excessively controlling and almost indifferent to their children's need for support and affection; one real concern in this style is the tendency toward physical punishment without appropriate and balancing support and affection. Particularly permissive parents (lower left-hand quadrant) would exhibit opposite tendencies—little control and overresponsiveness —allowing the wants and needs of the child to dictate home life. Very neglectful parents (lower right-hand quadrant) offer little direction to their children nor do they offer much support or affection. In Baumrind's work, authoritative parents (upper left-hand quadrant) offer the best blend of control and responsiveness.[34]

Dozens of studies have been conducted over the past several decades correlating these parenting styles with various social, behavioral, academic, and spiritual outcomes in children and adolescents.[35] More recently, a meta-analysis of parenting styles research focused on religious and spiritual outcomes in children.[36] This study suggests that the authoritative parenting style nurtures children spiritually better than other parenting styles. The warmth, love, responsiveness, and support of this parenting style, along with appropriate boundary setting, directive engagement, and discipline, offer a balanced approach to parenting that correlates with healthy social, achievement, and behavioral outcomes as well as spiritual outcomes.[37]

Parents who encourage religious and spiritual conversations, who participate with children in religious activities or rituals, who model a congruent spiritual life before their children, and who parent lovingly yet firmly are nurturing their children spiritually—that is, these four parenting practices foster the three main relationships that make up the child's spirituality: they help a child regulate their feelings (child-self), they help a child lean into relationships around them (child-others), and

---

[34]Baumrind, "The Influence of Parenting."

[35]Baumrind, "The Discipline Controversy," overviews many of these studies.

[36]Sungwon Kim, "Parenting Styles and Children's Spiritual Development," in *Nurturing Children's Spirituality: Christian Perspectives and Best Practices*, ed. Holly C. Allen (Eugene, OR: Cascade, 2008).

[37]Kim, "Parenting Styles."

they help a child come to know the God who loves them, cares for them, and wants to know them (child-God).

CHILDREN'S SPIRITUALITY, PARENTING, AND RESILIENCE

Borgo wisely tells us that "adults can't always make things better; we can't fix the larger world or the inner world of a child." However, she continues, we can help children connect with "the One who can speak love to their fear."[38]

One of my students at John Brown University, Jenny Barton, grew up in Kenya. In 2007 through 2008, Kenya experienced a period of political and economic crisis. Jenny's family lived in Nairobi during this dangerous period. For several weeks, while random violence spread across the country, the children stayed home from school, their dad went out only infrequently to purchase food, and their houseworkers remained in the Bartons' home for safety. Jenny was seventeen at the time, and her younger brothers were fourteen and six. She tells how her parents managed this season of unrest, danger, and fear in their country:

> I am most thankful for the way my parents held our family together and guided us through that traumatic and uncertain time. Looking back as an adult, I realize that this was no easy task. Not only were they trying to manage their own fears and uncertainties, but they also had to handle the thoughts and emotions of three children who were at very different points in life during a situation that was completely new to them.
>
> As teenagers, my brother Michael and I were very aware of the events taking place around us. My parents allowed us to watch the news, but when we did, they watched with us. They didn't want to hide too much from us, but they knew the current situation was going to be difficult for us to work through. My parents assured us that our feelings and fears were valid and that we were not alone in what we were experiencing. When we asked, they would share their thoughts and feelings (though, looking back, I realize they probably didn't share the full extent of their emotions).
>
> My parents addressed the needs of my little brother somewhat differently from the way they supported Michael and me. Chris, who was six,

---

[38]Borgo, *Spiritual Conversations*, 29.

seemed more aware of his surroundings than his agemates; he asked a lot of questions, some far beyond his years. They didn't allow him to watch the news, but they allowed him to ask questions and would answer them; they protected him from the distressing details of the unfolding events, but they always made sure he knew his questions were heard and valid.

For all three of us, my parents did their best to keep daily routines as normal as they could and to include fun activities to help keep our minds off the circumstances. We ate most meals together, spent a lot of time in our backyard, and played games or watched movies together.

Our home was a safe space where communication was valued and encouraged. Yet the thing I am most grateful for is the way my parents, through their words and actions, made sure we knew God was with us, ever present, even in troubled times. Through family prayer times and devotions, we were reminded that even though we didn't know what the future held, God did, and we could find comfort in that. My parents leaned into Christ, held tight to his promises, and relied on their faith to give them the strength to get through each day.[39]

When trauma comes, children need their parents to exhibit the strength and fortitude that Jenny's parents did. Parents protect children from harmful details that might worry them, and they carry the weight of the trauma, danger, and ongoing unknowns while leaning into their belief that God is present, that he knows them by name, and that he will accompany them in hard hours, days, or weeks. Parents cover their children; that is what they do.

Masten says parents buffer the effects of a difficult circumstance; their very presence can be adequate buffering in the common troubles of life (e.g., inoculations, running out of gas). In more dangerous situations, beyond being present, the parent's facial expression and other body language are important. Masten cautions parents that terror is contagious and that they may inadvertently telegraph stress and fear to their children.[40] Calmness and an undisturbed countenance are also contagious.

---

[39]Personal communication, May 24, 2020. Used with permission from Jennifer Barton.
[40]Masten, *Ordinary Magic,* 211.

It is in these anxious moments that children and parents have formative conversations and participate in shared life-giving rituals, and these conversations and rituals foster resilience.[41] It is in these intense moments that children observe their parents exhibiting courage and faith. It is in these fraught moments that children are especially blessed by strong and loving parenting.

One last caveat. If the parents themselves are suffering from the event that has befallen their children, they will need support in order to be able to parent their children well. Chapter six on intergenerational experiences offers ways the body of Christ can surround parents and families in crisis.

CONCLUSION

Hundreds of participants in Christian Smith's research repeatedly and unequivocally indicated that their parents had the deepest and most profound influence on their spiritual lives.[42] Parents powerfully influence their children through engaging them in regular spiritual rituals, recognizing the importance of frequent ordinary conversations and activities, modeling a congruent life—spiritually and religiously—and parenting firmly yet lovingly. Parents can also model trust and faith to children when adversities come.

On January 17, 1991, my husband and I, along with our children—David, fourteen; Daniel, eight; and Bethany, five—were traveling from London to Nairobi, Kenya. Halfway through the flight, the British Airways pilot announced, "British and American forces have just bombed Baghdad." Our children asked several questions but did not seem overly concerned.

During our three weeks deep in the bush of Kenya, we listened to the (first) Gulf War coverage on BBC radio, then we began our return trip to the States. We had a long layover in London, and as we walked through the airport, large newspaper headlines were eye-level for Daniel, our astute, observant eight-year-old. The headlines shouted, "Governments Warn: Travelers, Stay Home" and "Fears of Attack Empty Airports."

---

[41]Borgo, *Spiritual Conversations*, 5.
[42]Smith, *Soul Searching*; Smith, *Souls in Transition*.

As we waited for our flight in the nearly deserted gate area, Daniel looked up at me with intense, questioning eyes. He asked, "What will happen if they shoot our plane down?"

I looked down at him, then over at our other children and my husband, and said in a quiet, Spirit-calmed voice, "Then, Daniel, we—all of us—will be ushered into the presence of God together."

He peered into my eyes, then looked at his brother and sister and dad, looked back at me, and said, "Okay."

That is all he said. But his body visibly relaxed, and he pulled out his current LEGO minicreation and set to work rearranging the pieces.

CHAPTER FIVE

Grandparenting, Children's Spirituality, and Resilience

My grandmother, Dessie Heater Imboden (1904–1979), was my first and greatest teacher. I stayed with her for two summers, when I was five and six, while my mother (her daughter) finished her university degree.

During those summers our days followed a similar pattern. Every morning we rose early and prepared an enormous lunch for Grandpa to take out to the cotton fields near Hickory Ridge, Arkansas. Then we would cook eggs, bacon, biscuits, and gravy for breakfast. Grandpa would leave for a day of work on his tractor or combine, and Grandma and I would begin the daily chores of washing dishes, sweeping the floor, gathering the eggs, feeding the chickens. Afterward Grandma washed clothes and hung them outside, then we ironed yesterday's wash. Grandma let me iron the (pre–permanent press) pillowcases and Grandpa's enormous handkerchiefs.

Around ten o'clock Grandma and I would go into the living room, where she would sit in her small gold chair, put her feet on the low padded ottoman, and reach beside the chair for the enormous Bible that always sat there. I would pull up a three-legged stool and sit at her feet and watch the minute hand go around the clock while she studied. It lasted one hour. I would stare at the oval-framed picture of Grandpa's

Some sections of this chapter were taken from Holly C. Allen with Heidi Oschwald, "God Across the Generations: The Spiritual Influence of Grandparents," in *Nurturing Children's Spirituality: Christian Perspectives and Best Practice*, ed. Holly C. Allen (Eugene, OR: Cascade, 2008), 267-85. Used by permission of Wipf and Stock Publishers, www.wipfandstock.com.

stern-faced mother, study the glass knickknacks in the bric-a-brac shelves on the wall, and follow the antics of the tiny blue butterflies on the clover outside the window.

At precisely eleven o'clock, Grandmother would close her Bible and ask if I was ready to play Parcheesi. We played for an hour, ate lunch, and then began the afternoon's chores—bringing in the clothes, watering the hydrangea bushes and peonies, and weeding the vegetable garden.

I remember those days with delight. But the hourlong Bible study stands out particularly in my memory. This legacy from my grandmother—time daily in the Word—is a wonderful heritage. The habit of daily Bible study has sustained me through the hardships that God has allowed in my own life.

Grandparents are very interested in sharing the wisdom of their years with grandchildren,[1] and part of that wisdom for some grandparents is passing on their faith. They want to influence their grandchildren morally, religiously, and spiritually.

A 2018 study reported that 37 percent of respondents named grandparents as key influencers in their faith.[2] This and other research is showing that grandparents can and in fact do play a surprisingly important role in the spiritual lives of their grandchildren. Grandchildren report that they see, notice, and are witness to the ways their grandparents live lives of faith before them. They are beneficiaries of the love that is bestowed on them, the grace and the blessing that grandparents pour over them. They receive and carry into their futures the experiences and memories of grandparents who knew God.

HOW GRANDPARENTS SPIRITUALLY AFFECT THEIR GRANDCHILDREN

This chapter draws its major themes from Vern Bengston's amazing cross-generational study regarding the strong spiritual influence of

---

[1]Joseph A. Weber and Anita G. Absher, "Grandparents and Grandchildren: A 'Memory Box' Course Assignment," *Gerontology & Geriatrics Education* 24, no. 1 (2003): 76.
[2]"How Faith Heritage Relates to Faith Practice," Barna, July 9, 2019, www.barna.com/research /faith-heritage-faith-practice. The participants in this study were self-identified Christians who said their faith was very important in their lives and had attended a worship service within the past month.

grandparents,[3] from five recent studies that examine the religious/ spiritual facet of the grandparent-grandchild relationship,[4] and from my interviews with forty children and their insights about their grand- parents.[5] The responses of the children and the grandparents in the various studies offer support for the claim that grandparents influence children's spirituality through their frequent prayers, their wonderful stories, their clear example, their quiet witness, their availability to share experiences of wonder, and their ability to lavish love, grace, and mercy over grandchildren in deep need of such gifts.

Prayer. An important question for the children in my interviews was, "Of all the people you know, who do you think knows God the best?" The

---

[3]Vern Bengston with Norella Putney and Susan Harris, *Families and Faith: How Religion Is Passed Down Across Generations* (New York: Oxford University Press, 2013). Bengston and his col- leagues have been conducting the largest-ever study of religion and family across generations over the past thirty-five years, repeatedly interviewing more than 3,500 individuals in 350 fami- lies. Bengston has reported on this study in dozens of articles and several books. *Families and Faith* is a comprehensive report of what the study has found. One of its ten chapters focuses directly on the powerful spiritual influence of grandparents on their grandchildren.

[4]Matthew D. Deprez, "The Role of Grandparents in Shaping Faith Formation of Grandchildren: A Case Study," *Christian Education Journal* 14, no. 1 (2017): 109-27; Sharon V. King et al., "The Religious Dimension of the Grandparent Role in Three-Generation African American House- holds," *Journal of Religion, Spirituality & Aging* 19, no. 1 (2006): 75-96. King et al. interviewed fifty-seven members of multigenerational households seeking to discern the ways African Amer- ican grandparents transmit their religious values to younger family members; Alan C. Taylor and Ryan M. Wise, "The Influence of Grandparents on Grandchildren's Value Formation: Assessing the Perspectives of Grandparents and Grandchildren," *The Gerontologist (Program Abstracts: 57th Annual Scientific Meeting)* 44, no. 1 (2004): 86-98. Taylor and Wise asked ninety undergraduate students with at least one living grandparent to complete a questionnaire assessing their under- standing of their grandparents' influence on the formation of their values; the students then gave a similar questionnaire to their grandparent(s) (with 148 grandparents participating), assessing the grandparents' perception of their influence on their grandchildren's value formation; Weber and Absher, "Grandparents and Grandchildren." In this 2003 study, one hundred grandparents were interviewed to explore the types of memories they would like to leave with their grandchil- dren, many of which were religious/spiritual in nature; Valarie King and Glen H. Elder, "Are Religious Grandparents More Involved Grandparents?" *Journal of Gerontology: Social Sciences* 54B (1999): S317-28. King and Elder interviewed 585 grandparents to examine how various as- pects of their religious lives were related to involvement with their grandchildren.

[5]Interviews conducted as field research for Holly J. Allen, "A Qualitative Study Exploring the Similarities and Differences of the Spirituality of Children in Intergenerational and Non- Intergenerational Christian Contexts" (PhD diss., Biola University, 2002). In 2006, Heidi Schultz and Micah Siebert, students at John Brown University where I was teaching at the time, analyzed and coded the 250 pages of raw data collected from my interviews with forty children, focusing particularly on what the children said about their grandparents. Since the original purpose of the dissertation had not focused on grandparents per se, the raw data had not been fully analyzed in light of children's comments about their grandparents.

children had opportunity to name three or four different people who they thought knew God well. Altogether the children named 135 people. Besides mentioning parents, friends, friends' parents, pastors, Sunday school teachers, and other relatives, ten of the children said their grandmothers knew God, and four children named their grandfathers.

In my interviews, when children named someone they thought knew God, the next question was, "What is it about that person that makes you think he (or she) knows God?" In regard to grandparents knowing God, the children said things such as:

- The grandparent mentions God in birthday cards.
- The grandparent practices a daily quiet time with God.
- The grandparent is loving like God is.
- The grandparent shows faith in God in times of stress such as natural disasters.
- The grandparent brings gifts.

However, in describing why they think their grandmother or grandfather knew God, the most common answer was connected to the grandparent's prayer life. Eve (age ten) responded, "She [my grandmother] prays for everybody a lot." When asked how she knew her grandmother prayed for everybody, Eve said, "Sometimes she tells me and sometimes you just know." Nathaniel (age ten) also mentioned his grandmother as someone who knew God: "She's the best prayer warrior I know. She's been faithful all my life to prayer; she spends a very long time every day in prayer."[6]

Benjamin (age eleven) mentioned one of his grandfathers, saying, "He helps me go to the Lord. He and my dad help me go to the Lord, as does my mom. He was praying for me a lot." Benjamin also added about his grandmother: "She's very strong in prayer; when she was sick we would pray for her, she would pray for us, and she would pray for herself after she had prayed for everybody else that she knew of."[7]

The grandchildren in another study also testified to the influence of their grandparent on their prayer lives. Allison said, "I have watched my

---

[6]Allen, interviews conducted for "A Qualitative Study."
[7]Allen, interviews conducted for "A Qualitative Study."

grandmother bring the family together. I have learned to pray from her. She and my great-grandmother, they are prayer warriors."[8] The grandparents in this study reported they believed that praying for their grandchildren was a primary way they influenced their grandchildren.[9] The statements the children made about their grandparents in this study as well as in my field research support these grandparents' beliefs.

Stories. Grandparents typically take the role of providing continuity and passing down family stories and traditions very seriously.[10] Though I have recognized for some time that families need to be telling their stories, this conviction was confirmed when I read Jerome Berryman's description of suicidal children and their families:

> I worked at Houston Child Guidance Center from 1983 to 1985 as part of an interdisciplinary team that cared for suicidal children and their families. The team included a psychiatrist, a psychologist, a social worker, a medical doctor, drug expert, and myself, an Episcopal priest. We provided family systems therapy and studied what had gone wrong in the relationships that resulted in children trying to kill themselves. What these families had in common was that they did not tell stories. They did not tell stories about vacations, funny things that happened, sad things, grandparents, births, deaths, pets, hopes, trips, dreams, or any other tales I took for granted, since I had come from a storytelling family. Their communication was reduced to commands, demands, exclamations, brief explanations, and questions requiring short, factual answers. The family members were like neighboring islands without any bridges. There was no narrative to connect them. What was the treatment? We set up ways to encourage them to tell stories face-to-face.[11]

The children I interviewed interspersed their responses to questions with stories about their grandparents. In response to the question, "And what about someone who knows God; what does that look like?" Hannah (age eleven) shared this powerful story:

---

[8]King et al., "Religious Dimension of the Grandparent Role," 86.
[9]King et al., "Religious Dimension of the Grandparent Role."
[10]Weber and Absher, "Grandparents and Grandchildren," 76.
[11]Jerome W. Berryman, *Stories of God at Home* (New York: Church Publishing, 2018), 22.

My grandmother, they were in a tornado when they lived in Texas, and they [had] just become Christians and they went in the hallway and said, "Oh, we need some blankets and things." But they didn't have a chance to get anything, and when the tornado was over, everything was gone but the hallway. And grandmother said, "You [God] can do this, and I have faith in you."[12]

Benjamin (age eleven) explained that his grandfather knew the Lord and that he had been raised in China: "He was born there and stayed there for eleven years. He explains to me stuff about when he was there. He helps me go to the Lord."[13] His grandmother, someone else he named who knew God, had also shared experiences from her life with him, especially of the years she taught children in the Middle East and how she led some of those children to faith. Through the stories the grandparents told them over the years, the children were able to see that their grandparents knew God.

Stories act as mechanisms through which grandparents can teach succeeding generations how to live lives consistent with family and religious values.[14] Personal stories add meaning and coherence to their grandchildren's lives and offer structures on which to frame their experiences. Grandparents carry in their very being a sense of history that even their own children, their grandchildren's parents, may not yet have grasped.[15]

Grandparents as models. The Barna research in *The Spiritually Vibrant Home* mentions that grandparents tend to be more intentional than parents in leading spiritual interactions.[16] Grandparents may see themselves as Lois in Paul's words to Timothy: "I am reminded of your sincere faith, which first lived in your grandmother Lois and in your mother Eunice and, I am persuaded, now lives in you also" (2 Timothy 1:5). They often feel called to be role models, sharing with grandchildren

---

[12]Allen, interviews conducted for "A Qualitative Study."
[13]Allen, interviews conducted for "A Qualitative Study."
[14]Rockey Robbins, Avraham Scherman, Heidi Holeman, and Jason Wilson, "Roles of American Indian Grandparents in Times of Cultural Crisis," *Journal of Cultural Diversity* 12, no. 2 (2005): 62-68.
[15]Weber and Absher, "Grandparents and Grandchildren."
[16]Don Everts, *The Spiritually Vibrant Home: The Power of Messy Prayers, Loud Tables, and Open Doors* (Downers Grove, IL: InterVarsity Press, 2020), 94-95, 126.

the importance of "spiritual values, family heritage, education, and work ethic."[17]

Perhaps the most important contribution a grandparent can make is modeling faith.[18] Children learn how to act and live through the examples of the adults in their lives. In one study, Mia (age fifteen) says, "My grandfather's example has made us all. He was a Christian, and his example has shown us that it is possible for us to lead a close-to-perfect life. It is really big to us."[19] Boaz (age eleven) in describing why he thinks his grandfather knows God, says:

> Well, he usually talks about the Bible or stuff he has heard on the radio about God, and if one of us says something [that leads to] something he can say about God, he says it. He has a bunch of versions of the Bible. He's a really nice guy. You can kind of just tell. You know how in classes and stuff when you were young, people would say, "You're with God" and people could see the light in you; that's pretty much it.[20]

Vern Bengston's book *Families and Faith: How Religion is Passed Down Across Generations* attests to the influence of grandparents living their faith before their grandchildren.[21] For example, Bengston shares the story of Shari, who, though she did not feel close to her own parents, had a warm relationship with her grandfather that developed during a difficult childhood. Shari reported to Bengston that she saw her grandfather living his faith daily: "He didn't just go to church or talk about it; he actually lived the tenets of the faith. He was like a rock for me. You know, when everything was going bad, he was the rock."[22]

Betty Cloyd offers the following story of a man who lived a long distance from his grandson:

> [On a recent visit], the little boy was waiting at the window for him, as always. After they greeted each other, the little boy noticed that his grandfather

---

[17]Weber and Absher, "Grandparents and Grandchildren," 76.

[18]Robert J. Banks, "Grandparenting," in *The Complete Book of Everyday Christianity*, ed. Robert J. Banks and R. Paul Stevens (Downers Grove, IL: InterVarsity Press, 1997), 466.

[19]King et al., "Religious Dimension of the Grandparent Role," 86.

[20]Allen, interviews conducted for "A Qualitative Study."

[21]Bengston, *Families and Faith*.

[22]Bengston, *Families and Faith*, 106.

had on a baseball cap. The little boy ran quickly to his room and got his own cap and put it on. Then they sat down together in a rocking chair with the grandfather holding his grandson. The grandfather's feet were tired after his long trip, so he reached down and untied his shoes and took them off. Then he set them neatly, side by side, beside the chair. The little boy observed this, and then he too untied his shoes, took them off, and set them neatly beside his grandfather's. The grandfather said that he realized at that moment how important his presence was to his grandchild and how his life must always reflect the life that he wanted his grandson to emulate.[23]

As Irene Endicott says in her beautiful tribute *Grandparenting by Grace*, "Children imitate those they love the most. Everything we do and say around a grandchild risks mimicking."[24]

Of course, grandparents sometimes have a negative influence on their grandchildren. Robert Banks notes that "some grandparents embrace life, deal constructively with their losses, and maintain a sense of optimism and hope. Others become negative, are critical of the oncoming generation, and cover life, family, and community with a blanket of darkness."[25] And children notice; they pick up on these attitudes.

One of the questions asked in my field research interview was, "What is the difference between someone who knows God and someone who knows about God?" Esther (age nine) answered, "My grandma and grandpa on my dad's side don't know God, but my grandma and grandpa on my mom's side do know God and have a strong relationship with God." When asked, "So what is the difference?" she continued, "Those grandparents [Dad's parents] don't have the friendly relationship with God that my mom's parents have. I think they have Jesus in their head, but they don't have him in their heart."[26]

Nathaniel (age ten) said of his dad's dad, "He was an angry man. He divorced with my grandma. . . . He's an angry man."[27] These vignettes

---

[23]Betty S. Cloyd, *Parents and Grandparents as Spiritual Guides* (Nashville: Upper Room Books, 2000), 105-6.

[24]Irene M. Endicott, *Grandparenting by Grace* (Nashville: Broadman & Holman, 1994), 53.

[25]Banks, "Grandparenting," 465.

[26]Allen, interviews conducted for "A Qualitative Study."

[27]Allen, interviews conducted for "A Qualitative Study."

indicate that children do not automatically think grandparents are simply wonderful; they discern hypocrisy and unkind behavior, and they recognize ungodly behavior when they see it.

The conclusion of a 2017 study of the spiritual influence of grandparents sums it up well: "To have the best opportunity in shaping your grandchild's faith formation, practice your own faith passionately, consistently, and publicly so they can see how Christ has transformed you."[28]

Sharing unhurried time. Children crave attention and love. When grandparents take time to sit, play, or just enjoy their grandchildren, it helps children understand they are loved, cared for, and appreciated. When grandparents allow for this unhurried time to happen, a special bond develops between the child and grandparent.

In *The Spiritual Child*, Lisa Miller says, "Very often a grandparent becomes [a] special spiritual partner even when the parents are healthy and functional and spiritually supportive. In our busy lives, so often it is a grandparent who sits and listens to a child's questions, welcomes a child's feelings, and has the long deep talks at the kitchen table."[29]

My sister tells the following story that illustrates a bonding time she experienced with Jade, one of her grandchildren:

> When Cyrus was born, Grandma Gena (GG) came to visit. At dawn, four-year-old Jade got up and came downstairs where GG was rocking Jade's brand-new baby brother. Cyrus was snorting as new babies often do. GG was concerned the snorting might be alarming Jade, so she started talking about how Cyrus had much to learn since he came out of his mommy. GG whispered:
>
>> Cyrus' lungs are learning to breathe air for the first time. . . .
>> His eyes are learning to see for the first time in the light. . . .
>> His arms are learning to stretch to their fullest. . . .
>> His heart is learning—
>
> GG was going to say that Cyrus's heart was learning to pump his blood, but Jade interrupted and whispered in her sweet little voice, "His

---

[28]Deprez, "The Role of Grandparents," 109-27.
[29]Lisa Miller, *The Spiritual Child: The New Science on Parenting for Health and Lifelong Thriving* (New York: St. Martin's Press, 2015), 80.

heart is learning to love." GG retells this story when she and Jade are together, and this intimate moment continues to inform their close and loving relationship.

Grandparents can be people who allow children to reveal themselves emotionally and feel reassured that they are loved.[30] Jennie Hansen re-members the special bond that developed with her grandfather:

> I recall the feel of holding his hand as we walked down the street, watching his intense mischievous eyes, and his walking me home from the res-taurant at nights when my parents were still hard at work. There is a special trust and comfort that I had with him and a sense that he was old, yet not really. He was a part of my young life that became memorable, and perhaps that is in some measure why I have been so committed to inter-generational activity to assure that continuity of caring and value from one generation to the next.[31]

Knowing that grandparents care for them as individuals helps children develop as whole people.

Robert Atchley talks about the daily time his grandmother spent with him reading Bible stories:

> For my fifth birthday (in 1944), Granny gave me *The Golden Book of Bible Stories*, a large, thick book with deep blue binding, big print, and beautiful color prints depicting biblical scenes. We were living in a small city in the North Carolina mountains then, and the weather was chilly and dreary a lot that fall. We had a wide cast-iron grate in the living-room fireplace, where we burned huge chunks of coal to warm the small brick house. Granny and I got in the habit of sitting close together on the overstuffed horsehair couch, and in the flickering light she would read aloud those exciting and inspiring stories. We did this just about every day, and by my sixth birthday I could read them to her.[32]

Atchley's grandmother not only gave him a gift but also spent dedicated time with her grandchild almost every day, reading and teaching him about the different characters and events in the Bible.

---

[30]Robbins et al., "Roles of American Indian Grandparents," 62.
[31]Jennie C. Hansen, "Grandparents Remembered," *Generations* 20, no. 1 (1996): 75.
[32]Robert C. Atchley, "Grandparents Remembered," 71.

Many of the comments in research reveal that children appreciate the time their grandparents have spent with them just talking, reading the Bible or stories together, or praying together. The accounts that Hansen, Atchley, Grandma Gena, and the research participants share support the idea that those special unplanned quality times grandparents spend with their offspring can and do affect the spiritual lives of their grandchildren.

Spoiling and blessing. Two themes that appear in the popular literature about grandparents are the concepts of spoiling and blessing. Stephen and Janet Bly offer a new perspective on spoiling; they actually advocate spoiling one's grandchildren. They say, "To spoil implies giving someone better than he or she deserves. Every kid needs a bit of that. The Bible is crammed with accounts of how God spoils us—that is, gives us better than we deserve. It's called grace."[33]

Bly and Bly also highlight the concept of blessing in Genesis 48:9-28, where Jacob blesses his sons, in particular Joseph's sons, his grandsons Manasseh and Ephraim. A blessing can be as simple as reading a passage over a grandchild, for example: "I pray that you . . . [may know] 'how wide and long and high and deep is the love of Christ'" (Ephesians 3:18), or "The Lord bless you and keep you; the Lord make his face shine on you . . . and give you peace" (Numbers 6:24-26); or it can be the grandparent's own words, for example: "May you be true and faithful like Joshua and Daniel [or Esther and Ruth]; may you follow God all the days of your life," or "God is going before you; God has prepared you well for this good work." Blessing grandchildren can have a powerful, positive impact on them by demonstrating grace and love that aren't just the result of good behavior but are bestowed simply because the grandchildren are loved.

The children in most studies do not actually use the words "spoil" or "bless"; however, these concepts are embedded in some of their comments. Phoebe (age eleven) said of her grandmother, "When we are somewhere out [like playing ball], she will try her hardest to be down here for me whenever I need her."[34] Nathaniel (age ten) said that though

---

[33]Stephen A. Bly and Janet C. Bly, *The Power of a Godly Grandparent* (Kansas City: Beacon Hill Press, 2003), 30.

[34]Allen, interviews conducted for "A Qualitative Study."

his grandmother wasn't wealthy, if he wanted to go out to eat for a special occasion, "then I ask her and she will probably say yes. She's willing to do it for me."[35] And Myra (age twelve) says:

> [My grandparents] are so proud and enthusiastic about us. Not more than my parents, of course, but I guess they show it more. I'll tell you, I don't know what I did to have them love me and make such a fuss about me. It's almost embarrassing sometimes—I mean, when I'm around my friends— but I really love it.[36]

GRANDPARENTS, SPIRITUALITY, AND RESILIENCE IN CHILDREN

As established in chapter two, resilience research connects faith, hope, belief, religious commitment, prayer, and spiritual support to resilience in children. Grandparents who practice their faith before their grandchildren, particularly as they live out the arduous process of aging, can provide a model their grandchildren can draw on, even emulate, when they face adversity. Another resilience factor Masten outlined—the importance of close, loving, supportive relationships with people other than parents—comes into play in the grandchild-grandparent relationship. The following quote from Borgo illustrates well the confluence of both of these factors:

> Often, the most tangible example of unconditional love to a child is their relationship with a loving grandparent. The attention and care that grandparents offer to children has the potential to shape a loving and attentive image of God in the mind and heart of a child. Grandparents can embody a slower posture, which frees them up for endless listening with delight to children. Further, they embody timeworn wisdom and humility through which children sense an authentic love and generosity.[37]

Teachers, ministers, even peers sometimes fill this role, but grandparents—with their distinctive combination of kinship, continuing

---

[35] Allen, interviews conducted for "A Qualitative Study."
[36] Arthur Kornhaber and Kenneth L. Woodward, *Grandparents/Grandchildren: The Vital Connection* (Garden City, NY: Doubleday, 1981), 12.
[37] Borgo, *Spiritual Conversations,* 27.

presence, and maturity—uniquely supply that close, stable support that can help sustain children when life falls down.

Cloyd writes tenderly about the impact her grandfather had on her and the other children in her family:

> My grandfather, a devout man who lived his faith daily, greatly influenced my life. Often my grandfather would gather his grandchildren around him for a time of prayer and for reading the scripture. He would take us in his arms and say to us, "Remember, now, you belong to God and God loves you very much."[38]

These grandchildren realize they are loved and cared for not only by their grandparents, but also by God.

CONCLUSION

The children in these studies attest to the fact that they see, they notice, they are witness to the ways their grandparents live lives of steadfast faith before them. They are beneficiaries of the love that is bestowed on them, the grace and the blessing that grandparents pour over them. The time they spend with loving, caring, believing grandparents nurtures their relationships with themselves, others, and God.

It has been forty years since I said goodbye to my grandmother; no one in my life has influenced me more than she. I have carried with me throughout life the experiences and memories of my time with her. She knew God, she lived before me a congruent life, she endured hardship with fortitude and steadfastness, she trusted God, and she had a deep hope, a hope I carry forward today, the hope that I will see her again and we will once again praise Jesus together.

---

[38]Cloyd, *Parents and Grandparents*, 25.

PART THREE

Churches, Children's Spirituality, and Resilience

CHAPTER SIX

Intergenerational Christian Experiences

IN THE MID-2000s, ten years after our first experiences in an inter-generational church, my family was once again part of a small church plant that met in intergenerational small groups every Sunday evening with babies, children, teens, emerging adults, young adults, middle adults, and senior adults all together. During a discussion about persecution at one of our gatherings, Kelsey, a seventh grader at the time, asked the group for some advice. She told us that her classmates had been harassing her about her beliefs and that recently she had pushed back at them, saying, "I can believe what I want." Kelsey then asked the group how she should answer those around her who challenge her faith.

The response of the group was multilayered and supportive. One of the high school students in our group offered encouraging words; two ninth-grade boys listened with keen interest; two elementary boys sitting on the floor also followed the conversation closely; a grandmother in the group offered support and insight; one of the parents in the group did also. The two preschoolers were playing with toys in the middle of our circle, but their eyes and ears were attuned.

Portions of this chapter are adapted from Holly C. Allen, "Reshaping the Church into an Inter-generational Body," in *Along the Way: Conversations About Children and Faith,* ed. Ron Bruner and Dana Kennamer Pemberton (Abilene, TX: Abilene Christian University Press, 2015), 95-110, used by permission of Abilene Christian University Press; and from Holly C. Allen, "No Better Place: Fostering Intergenerational Christian Community" in *Shaped by God: 12 Essentials for Nurturing Faith in Children, Youth, and Adults,* ed. Robert Keeley (Grand Rapids, MI: Faith Alive Christian Resources, 2010), 109-25.

Later when the group gathered in a standing circle, holding hands, Kelsey's dilemma was lifted in prayer; I was watching during the prayer to take in the response of the group. I noticed that a couple of the teens nodded during that part of the prayer. Three-year-old Matthew had placed his hand in his grandfather's hand but had not offered his other hand to Kelsey, who was standing next to him. During the prayer Matthew peered intently at each person in the group, working his way around the entire circle. When Kelsey's name was brought up, Matthew peeked up at her, touched her arm, and, as she opened her fingers, slipped his small hand into hers as they shared a small, shy smile.

In this gathering all of us were participating in the spiritual formation of both Kelsey and Matthew. This type of intergenerational care and nurture was common in our small groups at that time, but in general, this type of informal intergenerational ministry is uncommon in contemporary American Christianity—for the simple and obvious reason that the generations are rarely together in order for intergenerational ministry to occur.

HOW DO INTERGENERATIONAL SETTINGS NURTURE CHILDREN SPIRITUALLY?

During the last hundred years our society has begun to systematically separate families and segregate generations. Among the societal changes that have contributed to pervasive age segregation are age-graded public education, the movement from extended to nuclear family, the prevalence of preschools for the young, and retirement communities and assisted care facilities for older persons.

Churches have been among the few places where all generations come together on a consistent interactive basis. Yet the societal drift toward age separation has moved into churches over the past few decades. Age-based Bible classes for children (as well as adults), youth ministry programs, and separate worship services for adults, youth, and children tend to separate families and age groups from each other. Perennially separating the generations in this way could mean that children would experience Christian community in an age-segregated way throughout their lives.

What do children miss if they are perpetually with those their own age? And what do they gain when they intermingle with other generations?

Nurturing the child-God relationship. Some years ago I interviewed forty children from two different types of church settings: (1) intergenerational churches, where children met regularly in cross-generational small groups, and (2) non-intergenerational churches, where children were almost always segregated from adults.[1]

In the interviews I asked the children questions such as: Who do you know who knows God? What is it about that person that makes you think they know God? What does it mean to know God? Do you know God?

Toward the end of the interview I asked the children: Do you talk to God? What sorts of things do you talk to God about? Do you ever listen to God? In what ways does God talk to us? Have you ever thought God talked to you?

More than any of their other comments on a particular practice or subject, the children's remarks about prayer shed light on the depth and quality of their spiritual lives. Also, this area yielded the largest differences between the two groups. Children in both settings (intergenerational and non-intergenerational) spoke of prayer frequently, said they knew God, and described knowing God similarly. However, the children from the intergenerational settings were more aware of their relationship with God—that is, a larger number of them spoke more frequently and exhibited relationality in more of their discussions of prayer than did the children from non-intergenerational settings.[2]

Why might this be so?

Typically, in intergenerational small groups, adults, teens, and children pray for each other—as the opening story illustrates. They pray for ordinary concerns such as relational difficulties, job issues, and school

---

[1]The interviews were part of the field research for my dissertation: Holly J. Allen, "A Qualitative Study Exploring the Similarities and Differences of the Spirituality of Children in Intergenerational and Non-Intergenerational Christian Contexts" (PhD diss., Biola University, 2002).

[2]Holly C. Allen, "Nurturing Children's Spirituality in Intergenerational Settings," *Lutheran Educational Journal* 139 (Winter 2003): 118. To determine whether the difference between the two groups of children was statistically significant, I tallied the number of times a participant mentioned prayer (before the questions about prayer were asked) and then performed statistical comparison. The t-test was significant: $t(38)=2.37$, $p=.02$.

problems, and they pray for transitions such as new babies, graduations, and job changes. Over time, as the group participants grow closer, they pray over miscarriages, job losses, fears, hopes, and dreams. The children in my research who had participated in intergenerational small groups had experienced on a regular basis adults, teens, and other children in their lives praying for them, and they had learned to pray for others as well.

One story keenly illustrates the changes that can occur in everyone over months of praying for one another in intimate small groups. In preparation for my doctoral program back in the 1990s, I took several graduate courses in Bible, Christian education, and theology. The first course I took was New Testament Theology with one of the toughest professors in the seminary; I rose at five one morning to study for the initial test in the course. When our son Daniel (about thirteen at the time) got up around six-thirty, he found me going through my notes and asked me what I was working on. I told him I had studied for a test until midnight, that I was forgetting more than I was remembering, and that I was fearful I would make a poor showing. When I finished explaining how I was feeling, Daniel looked at me for a moment, then asked, "Do you want me to pray for you?"

Daniel had been learning experientially in the small groups that the first thing to do is pray. And that is what he did. He sat beside me on our blue couch and prayed for me. It was a deeply moving moment for us, a bonding moment, a memorable event in our relationship.

As mentioned previously, the most significant difference between the two groups of children in my research was in the area of prayer. The children who met regularly in intergenerational small groups referred to prayer *significantly* more often than did the children from non-intergenerational settings. So if we believe that prayer nurtures spiritual growth and development, especially the child-God relationship, we will want our children to be in settings where prayer is pervasive, where they hear other believers pray in warm, close settings, and where they begin to see that this is the first place to go when facing challenges in life.

Nurturing the child-others relationship. Our working definition of children's spirituality includes the child's relationship with self, others, and

God. The *others* aspect of children's spirituality is nurtured through parents, of course, but even more fully in intergenerational faith community settings. Children are saturated there with the *others* component of spirituality.

Experiences in small intergenerational gatherings contribute not only to a child's relationship with God but also to the child's relationships with others. Recently the leader of a small group played a worship video and asked everyone to think of something beautiful or something for which they were thankful; the song played was "This is Love" by New Wine Worship. During the song, which lasted five minutes, an eight-year-old moved to the floor, a ten-year-old sat in her chair with her eyes closed, a four-year-old went from lap to lap, and a two-year-old played with a puzzle. After the video, the group members responded with the following ideas that they found beautiful or for which they were thankful: "for being a Christian" (ten-year-old); "that I have so much love in my life" (her dad); "the presence of God is so awesome, I never want to be without his presence" (single dad); "that he healed me and my son" (leader); "I'm grateful for the healing and deliverance I have experienced at this church" (older single man); "for my mom feeling better about the divorce and she's getting better" (eight-year-old); "for God's healing power," "that I don't participate in the gossip at work anymore," and "I have a new boldness and the girls at work are asking me to pray for them" (thirtysomething).

Participating in this kind of authentic interchange can help children come to know God and come to know others around them who are also coming to know God.

In the earlier research I cited, when I asked the children, "Who do you know who knows God?" the children often responded by naming their parent or parents, but the children also mentioned dozens of others. One intriguing finding was that eight of the boys (out of nineteen) mentioned a friend's father as someone they knew who knew God. Typically, it is difficult for children to know very much about the spiritual lives of their friends' fathers. So why did these children give this answer? Turns out that all eight of the boys met in small intergenerational groups on a regular basis.[3] For

---

[3]Allen, interviews conducted for "A Qualitative Study."

instance, Stephen, eleven, describing his friend's dad, says, "Every time he will come up and greet me as if we were just equal people, and I've seen him praying before; he's a very deep and wonderful Christian actually. He's a great example for everybody."[4]

Children see God in others' lives, they experience others' spirituality, and they come to know God better through these interactions. How children see their parents, other adults in their lives, teens, and other children influences their perception of God. Children see God in relation to others in their Christian community, and they begin to pursue him and experience him personally in light of what they observe and experience not only in their homes but among the whole community of believers.

Albert Bandura's decades-long work in social learning theory has emphasized the crucial role of observation as children (and others) learn a culture's way of being and as they develop their values.[5] Bandura says that people do not need to learn everything through direct experience, since acquiring new ways of being, new knowledge, and new values only by trial and error would be problematic and time consuming. Fortunately, human beings can learn many things through observation and modeling. In his most recent work, Bandura extends his social learning theory into the spiritual realm, centering on the important role of modeling in transmitting spiritual beliefs and practices.[6]

Bandura relates several social modeling concepts to spiritual modeling. For instance, he notes that abstract social principles alone are typically poorly applied—that is, people need concrete examples of these principles to understand them and practice them.[7] For example, parents may tell children to be thoughtful of others' needs, and when their children see a parent take a meal to an elderly ailing neighbor, they experience a

---

[4]Allen, interviews conducted for "A Qualitative Study."

[5]Albert Bandura, *Social Foundations of Thought and Action: A Social Cognitive Theory* (Englewood Cliffs, NJ: Prentice Hall, 1986); Albert Bandura, "A Social Cognitive Theory of Personality," in *Handbook of Personality: Theory and Research*, 2nd ed., ed. Lawrence A. Pervin and Oliver P. John (New York: Guilford, 1999); Albert Bandura, "Social Cognitive Theory: An Agentic Perspective," *Annual Review of Psychology* 52 (2001): 1-26.

[6]Albert Bandura, "On the Psychosocial Impact and Mechanisms of Spiritual Modeling," *International Journal for the Psychology of Religion* 13, no. 3 (2003).

[7]Bandura, "On the Psychosocial Impact and Mechanisms of Spiritual Modeling."

concrete example of caring. Bandura connects this concept to spirituality by noting that doctrinal abstracts are likewise difficult to grasp concretely.[8] Faith communities offer many examples of those who live their lives in ways that embody their theological beliefs. For example, in my childhood I knew two committed believers who told stories of what it had been like to be a pacifist during World War II. These strong people demonstrated to me very tangibly what it meant to live a life devoted to God and to believe without a doubt that this world is not our real home.

Intergenerational Christian settings provide spiritual models up and down the age spectrum for children to observe and ultimately to emulate on their own formative spiritual journeys. When children have listening companions who hear, acknowledge, and encourage their early experiences with God, Borgo says this "creates a spiritual footprint that will shape the way a child engages with God, others, and themselves."[9]

Nurturing the child-self relationship. When I read articles or research by those deeply involved in family ministry, I find that they typically view the role of the nuclear family (in various forms) as the *primary* place where children are formed into Christ, where they construct a worldview, and where they find their identity.

I recognize that the inherent lifelong influence of the family of origin on children is undeniable. Yet I believe that a more holistic biblical and theological understanding is this: spiritual development, character, worldview, morality—that is, all of our basic personal, social, relational, and spiritual ways of being—are to be formed principally in our faith communities.

Another way to say this is that our primary identity should ultimately come not from our family of origin but from the body of Christ. The name on my birth certificate reads, "Holly Jeanean Catterton." I am a Catterton by birth; I am proud of my maiden name, and I love my family of origin. It has shaped me and continues to shape me in countless ways both identifiable and mysterious. To honor that important identity, I

---

[8]Bandura, "On the Psychosocial Impact and Mechanisms of Spiritual Modeling."
[9]Lacy Finn Borgo, *Spiritual Conversations with Children* (Downers Grove, IL: InterVarsity Press, 2020), 5.

have taken as my professional name Holly Catterton Allen, thus honoring my family. However, as important as my family of origin is to me, being a Catterton (and now also an Allen) is secondary to the fact that I am of Christ; I am a Catterton and an Allen, but most importantly, I am a Christ-follower, a Christian.[10]

Our place with Christ in the faith community is an integral part of our identity. It is there that we are shaped, conformed to the *imago Dei*. Just as David's identity was inherently embedded in the fact that he was part of God's people, a Hebrew of the tribe of Judah, our identities should be embedded in the fact that we are believers in Christ and therefore have been added by God to his church; we become part of a faith community that gathers to worship, minister, bless, and care for one another and others. And, as we know, having a strong sense of identity can be a stabilizing influence on children as they face adversity.

INTERGENERATIONAL CHRISTIAN EXPERIENCES, CHILDREN'S SPIRITUALITY, AND RESILIENCE

Intergenerational communities are unique places for children's spirituality to flourish if we describe spirituality as their relationship with themselves, others, and God. Inviting children into our settings, welcoming them, and hearing from them honors these children and enlightens the adults as well. "Children who have learned to listen to their inner life and orient that life in divine community have a[n] . . . inner compass that can guide them when the storms of life inevitably come. Spiritual conversations with children foster resiliency in the life of the child," Borgo states.[11]

One factor that contributes to a child's resilience, as Masten and others indicate, is being part of thriving community and cultural systems that encourage and support the child.[12] These systems provide ways for children to be connected to adults in their communities, adults who can be strong role models who demonstrate resilience in the face of adversity.

---

[10]This small section on identity is adapted from Holly C. Allen, "Family Ministry," in *Christian Education: A Guide to the Foundations of Ministry*, ed. Freddy Cardoza (Grand Rapids, MI: Baker Academic, 2019), 223-24.

[11]Borgo, *Spiritual Conversations*, 5.

[12]Ann Masten, *Ordinary Magic: Resilience in Development* (New York: Guilford Press, 2015).

Often these communities are churches. "Religious communities provide many opportunities for children to interact with adults and peers outside the family, people who the family approves because they share many of the same values. In a dangerous situation, these adults and peers can provide help, mentoring, and prosocial activities that foster competence and resilience in times of turmoil," according to Masten.[13]

When my friend J. P. Conway was eight years old, he and his family were on a road trip when a young driver in the other lane swerved into their 1985 Toyota. His mother was killed. The rest of the family survived, though his father experienced serious injuries. J. P. tells his story this way:

> I still remember the first thing I uttered when told of my mother's passing. For hours after the accident, I feared the worst. I kept asking nurses at the hospital for details of my mother, but they kept putting me off. Finally, I fell asleep in a hospital room with fluorescent lighting beside my brother. Hours later, they woke me up when my grandparents arrived from Tennessee. Alongside them, a chaplain broke the news I'd expected. And these are the words that came out of me: "Who will be my mother?"
>
> Somehow, I understood I needed a broader, larger family. Who would be my mother? My grandmother nurtured me in amazing ways. A few years later, my dad remarried, and my second mom has enriched my life in innumerable ways. Yet in my life, the answer to this question has been filled by a group larger than any one person. Over time, I realized this truth: the church had become my mother.
>
> I grew up at a very normal church of about three hundred or four hundred people. From an outside perspective, it probably would have looked ordinary. Yet for me, it was family.
>
> When I walked into my church building, I walked into a room full of uncles and aunts. In fact, I called many of them by those names, despite no blood relation. Everyone knew my name, and I knew their names. People smiled when they saw me. I loved being there. My childhood consisted of church potlucks, church cookouts, and church camp. I ran around with my friends and drank entirely too much Kool-Aid. On summer nights at church camp, we'd sing under the stars. It all felt so perfect, so Edenic. I

---

[13]Masten, *Ordinary Magic*, 255.

remember a song with this line: "Holy father, grant us peace." We'd sing it right before bed. I don't know how we sounded, but to my childish ears, it sounded like angels. Surprising to me, God was granting me peace. I missed my mom, and yet I had my people. I felt safe. I felt welcome. If you wonder what it's like to grow up with hundreds of people that think you're awesome and hug you weekly, I can tell you. It's incredible.[14]

J. P. is now a minister in Nashville, leading a midsized church that is intentionally intergenerational in outlook and practice. The children of this church are surrounded by "aunts" and "uncles" who know their names; everyone munches doughnuts together on Sunday morning before classes; the church carries out several all-generational service projects and mission trips every year. J. P.'s desire is that as these children walk their spiritual journeys with older and younger Christ-followers, they will receive love and care that will build in them the faith, hope, and resilience they will need as they move through life.

---

[14]I heard J. P. tell this story a few years ago at a ministry retreat; he has recently written a book in which he shares a much fuller version: Joseph P. Conway, *Broken but Beautiful* (Eugene, OR: Wipf & Stock, 2020), 3-5. Used by permission of Wipf and Stock Publishers, www.wipfandstock.com.

CHAPTER SEVEN

God's Story, Our Story

MY GRANDMOTHER WAS BORN IN 1904 in Olney, Illinois. Her name was Dessie Heater, and she had two younger sisters. Dessie's mother eventually gave birth to a baby boy, Charley, but she died in childbirth. The three little girls tried to care for their new little brother, but when Charley was six months old, he died from diarrhea and dehydration. My grandmother told me she didn't know what to do for him, nor did their dad, who worked most of the time. Not long after her mother and baby brother died, Dessie's dad died in a coal-mining accident, leaving the three little girls as orphans. Dessie was eleven years old.

In Dessie's community lived a young couple named William Christopher (W. C.) and Marian Abigail Nettleton Shake. They were in their early twenties and had been married only a few months. This young couple took in Dessie and her two sisters and raised them. Dessie had never seen a Bible or been inside a church building; it was through the Shakes that my grandmother first came to know the stories of the Bible. Through them she also came to know Jesus and was a well-loved member of her small rural church in Arkansas (where she moved after her marriage to my grandfather in the 1920s) until her death in 1979.

My grandmother's story has been very meaningful to me. I think of her character and how it was formed in those years when she lost her mother, her baby brother, and her father as a young girl. I think of how

Portions of this chapter were adapted from Holly C. Allen, "How Kids Grow Spiritually," in *Sunday School That Works! The Complete Guide to Maximize Your Children's Ministry Impact*, ed. Christine Yount Jones (Loveland, CO: Group Publishing, 2014), 29-36. Used by permission of Group Publishing.

she came to know God and put her hope and trust in him and how she lived that life of hope and faith before me.

I know the power of a story.

We are a story-formed people. God who made us knows that stories speak to us uniquely, and thus about half of Scripture is made up of story. This chapter invites parents, teachers, ministers, and other believers to winningly draw children into the biblical story with the purpose of helping them see God at work through the ages, bringing about his good purposes and delivering his people from their enemies. Indeed, God's work—that is, God's *story*—is continuing in God's followers through people like the Shakes and my grandmother, and even today through these very children. These children are part of God's people, part of God's work in the world, part of God's story. And telling Bible stories, that is, inviting children into God's story, can foster their relationships with God, others, and self, creating relationships that can form the foundation of a resilience in them that can last a lifetime.

TELLING BIBLE STORIES IN SUNDAY SCHOOL

For the past hundred years, many have viewed Sunday school as the primary means for fostering faith in our children. Over the last several decades, Christian faith traditions have constructed developmentally appropriate, biblically accurate, and (more recently) creative and exciting curricula for Sunday school and children's church; congregations have built magnificent facilities, employed one or more full-time children's ministers, and recruited armies of volunteers. Supporting smoothly functioning children's programs has been a top priority for many churches with a substantial line item in the church budget; church leaders believe they have a mandate to promote faith in the children of the church—and indeed I agree.

While the profession of children's ministry has matured, the field of children's spirituality has flourished as well, supported by rigorous cross-disciplinary research. Children's ministers and other church leaders are now asking how Sunday school or children's church programs can encompass spiritual development as well as the other purposes of faith development.

Nurturing children spiritually in our faith communities is a comprehensive task—much bigger than Sunday school. Sunday school cannot do everything. Mission trips can do things Sunday school cannot do well; parents model and live before their children in ways Sunday school teachers cannot; intergenerational small groups provide opportunities that age-specific Sunday schools cannot provide; worshiping together with the whole body of Christ blesses profoundly. But Sunday school does play a unique and powerful role in this crucial task of fostering children spiritually. So what does Sunday school do best?

Traditionally the goal of Sunday school has been to teach children the Bible. This is a very important and basic goal for Sunday school. However, a crucial question must be alloyed with this goal, and that question is this: *Why* do we teach children the Bible?

For years, I taught the Bible to children for two reasons: (1) so the children would come to know the Bible, and (2) so they would know how to live. And indeed, these are good reasons to teach the Bible—but they are not sufficient.

Now when I teach the Bible to children, my long-term, ultimate purpose is to help them *know God*—that is, my goal is to foster that ineffable child-God relationship. As I teach the Bible to reveal to children who God is, those other goals begin to come to fruition—that is, children come to know the Bible and they learn how to live—in response to who God is.

The child-God relationship. The aspect of children's spirituality that Sunday schools can contribute to the most is the child-God relationship. Sunday schools may also nurture the child-self and child-others relationships (addressed later), but a key responsibility of Sunday school is to teach children God's story in order to nurture that primary, crucial child-God connection.

Typically, Sunday school is the place where we lead children intentionally into the Christian metanarrative. A metanarrative is a grand narrative that explains a people group's history, experience, knowledge, purpose, and reason for being. The Christian metanarrative is God's story; it is the story that explains who God is, who we are (spiritual human beings made in the image of God, but fallen), where we came from (from God's mind and imagination), why we are here, and how we are to live as believers (to honor our Creator and to love others as God loves).

As children absorb God's master story, they come to see how God has related to his people through the ages and what God has been doing in that world. Whatever else we do in Sunday school, we must always ask, "What does this story (or this lesson) tell us about God?" That is, who is God and what is God doing? As we ask children week after week to respond to these questions, they will eventually be able to trace God's hand in history as he drew people—Abraham, Leah, Rahab, David, Josiah, Lydia, Saul/Paul—to himself and into his story. Along the way we can walk with children as they begin to see what God is doing in the world now and how he is drawing them into his story as well. Most importantly, these children will come to know God—not just know *about* him—and God will become their God. This relationship has been God's desire from the beginning, as he has expressed repeatedly throughout Scripture:

> I will claim you as my own people, and I will be your God. (Exodus 6:7 NLT)

> I will walk among you and be your God, and you will be my people. (Leviticus 26:12)

> So you will be my people, and I will be your God. (Jeremiah 30:22)

> I will put my laws into their minds
>   and write them on their hearts.
> I will be their God,
>   and they will be my people. (Hebrews 8:10)

And finally, one day in heaven:

> They will be his people, and God himself will be with them and be their God. (Revelation 21:3)

Thus, to nurture children spiritually, especially the child-God relationship, excellent Sunday schools will take as their primary goal ensuring that children indeed know God's master story because it is a primary way they will come to know God.

Sunday schools have traditionally done two other things that foster the child-God relationship: encouraging memory work and modeling and promoting prayer. Though memorizing Scripture seems to have fallen out of favor in recent years, placing God's Word in the hearts of our children gives them a powerful tool they can call on in times of need. The verses I memorized as a child have secured me in life's storms; when our beloved faith community was torn asunder and my husband lost his job twenty years ago, the future seemed desolate and empty. Romans 15:13 anchored my heart: "May the God of hope fill you with all joy and peace as you trust in him, so that you may overflow with hope by the power of the Holy Spirit." Words that had meant little to me when I memorized them as a child became life for me; as I spoke those words every day for two years, the God of hope held me fast.

Sunday schools have also been strong venues for modeling, encouraging, and promoting the child's active prayer life. Hearing Sunday school teachers and other children pray frequently and regularly gives children language to speak to God; children who grow up hearing only the more formal Sunday worship prayers may not feel they have an appropriate "voice" to speak to God. Of course, in some homes, mothers, fathers, and siblings regularly model and encourage prayer, but in many homes this practice is uncommon or absent. Thus listening to the prayers of boys, girls, and lay men and women offers children a variety of ways to converse with the God who is becoming their God.

The child-others relationship. Sunday schools contribute significantly to another component of children's spirituality by fostering the child's relationship with others who know God—both adults and peers. Probably most significantly, children come to know other adults who know and love God; Sunday school teachers have been profoundly influential role models for children for decades. Almost every adult Christian, if prompted, can immediately, often tearfully, express deep appreciation for one or more Sunday school teachers who were Jesus to them; even children who come from strong Christian homes benefit deeply from seeing Christ in adults who have been on the spiritual journey for decades. These cross-generational relationships contribute to children's spiritual growth and development in unique ways, and Sunday school is one of the few places where children have opportunities to regularly and personally interact with adult believers.

My story is connected to Edythe Lane, a mother of six children who taught the fifth and sixth grade girls' class at my church when I was a child. Unlike most of the other Sunday school teachers who read from the teacher book, Mrs. Lane talked from a deep well within her. She shared experiences with us in which she had leaned into her faith and even times when she had questioned God. The Old Testament stories she told us were full of drama and excitement. I began to realize that these stories were of real men and women who had actually lived, who exhibited strength and courage, who failed miserably, and who called on God in desperation.

A few years ago I had the honor of speaking at Edythe Lane's memorial service. I was able to acknowledge before the large gathering, which included her six children (and their children) and generations of children (now adults) who had sat at her feet, her powerful role in my life. As I spoke, I beheld an undulating wave of nodding heads to support my story.

Most adult Christians also have complex and layered memories of the children who shared their life and learning in Sunday school. They played Bible games with these children, memorized Scripture together, sang the books of the Bible together, and learned the stories together; perhaps they prayed together and cried together. They observed as other children accepted Christ and were baptized; they may have processed difficult theological questions together, such as "What happens to people who die who have never heard of Jesus?" Sometimes children just ahead of them on the journey influenced them profoundly, and often they became role models for those following behind. All of these relationships can nurture the child spiritually.

Scripture pervasively depicts Christianity as a communal enterprise. In other words, following God is not a solitary calling. God knows we need faith communities made up of believing "brothers" and "sisters," both older and younger, to foster our spiritual journeys. And Sunday schools are key places to develop these relationships that encourage spiritual formation.

The child-self relationship. Helping children come to know themselves has not been a focus or a strength of Sunday schools in the past, and I must confess that I do not think it is the primary responsibility of Sunday schools to do so. As stated earlier, I believe that the most important thing Sunday school can do is help children enter God's story, coming to know God as their God and seeing themselves as part of God's people. However, I do believe that the child-self relationship can be fostered along the way, especially since the child-self relationship is closely connected to the child-God relationship. Therefore, as the stories of God's work on earth are told, questions that nurture the child-self relationship can also be asked:

• What was Joseph afraid of? If I had been Joseph, what would I have feared? What do I fear now?

• Why might Jacob have loved Rachel more than Leah? How did Leah feel? Where did Leah eventually begin to place her trust? How am I like Leah? Have I ever felt less loved? Why is it so hard to believe that God's love is enough?

• Why did Rahab believe what she had heard about Yahweh and act on her belief by hiding the spies? If I consider myself in her place, what would have been my thoughts? Fears? Hopes?

• Consider John Mark when he found that Paul did not want to travel with him. What if I had been John Mark? How would I have felt? When I have failed, who has been my Barnabas? Who has believed in me?

These questions can be processed orally in class, allowing children to answer as they wish. The resulting discussions can become springboards for further self-examination and processing. However, offering them as personal "wondering" questions—that is, questions to think about, to contemplate, to wonder about—can offer children much-needed space to consider who they are and who they are becoming. By the questions we ask, we can encourage children in our Sunday school classes to begin to reflect on their own hearts, their own fears, and their own desires.

In general, Sunday schools have not allowed much space for stillness and contemplation; typically, few opportunities are provided for children to wonder about themselves or about God. Therefore, one recommendation I would make is that while telling God's story we incorporate times of reflection. In doing so we offer our children time to think, listen, and perceive—time to ask, "Who are you, Lord?" and "Who am I, Lord?"

CHILDREN'S SPIRITUALITY, STORY, AND RESILIENCE

A few years ago, Madison, one of my children's ministry majors, completed her internship with an orphanage in Uganda. Every day for two weeks, she and other workers told stories of children in the Bible. As Madison began to prepare these stories, she realized that many children in Scripture faced tremendously adverse circumstances—for example, Joseph and his kidnapping by his brothers and eventual sale into slavery; Miriam's role in watching her brother in the Nile; Samuel's childhood with Eli in the tabernacle away from his parents and siblings; the slave girl who was taken from Israel by Naaman's armies; Shadrach, Meshach, and Abednego; the epileptic boy Jesus healed; and all the Israelite children who left Egypt and wandered in the wilderness with their families.

Madison was surprised to realize how many children in Scripture were raised in situations where their parents were absent. After each story, she asked this question: "Who are you in this story?" The children of the orphanage found in Scripture children who were like them. The children in these Bible stories struggled, relied on God, and lived into a future brighter than might have been expected. Telling the stories of children in Scripture who suffered through difficult situations can provide comfort and encouragement to children who may be experiencing challenges and struggles themselves.[1]

Orphans, population-wide trauma survivors, chronically ill children, and refugees can relate in deep ways to the children of Scripture who

---

[1]Donald F. Walker, Jennifer Barsky Reese, John P. Hughes, and Melissa J. Troskie, "Addressing Religious and Spiritual Issues in Trauma-Focused Cognitive Behavior Therapy for Children and Adolescents," *Professional Psychology: Research and Practice* 41 (2010): 178.

endured, listened to stories about God, and told their own children about God's provision. Each time we tell one of these stories, we can ask questions that foster relationship (and resilience), such as:

- Who are you in this story?
- How are you like this child/person?
- How would you like to be like this child/person?
- How do you see God at work in this story?
- How do you see God at work in *your* story?

Helping children enter God's story fosters resilience in other ways as well. Children who are resilient tend to have a strong sense of identity and belonging.[2] As we help children find their place in God's story, as they begin to see themselves as someone God is calling, leading, and loving, as they begin to recognize that they—like David, Mary, Samuel, and Jairus's daughter—are loved, they begin to embrace their foundational identity as a child of God, as one who belongs to God.

There is a postscript to my grandmother's story. In the 1980s, I met a retired professor named Roy Shake. Roy and his wife, Bonnie, were well known in the city of Abilene, Texas, where they had been foster parents, caring for more than sixty children over three decades. Roy had been born and raised in Olney, Illinois. As it turned out, Roy had been the first biological child of W. C. and Abigail Shake, that loving couple who had taken in my grandmother and her sisters. Roy had known my grandmother. He told me he was five years old when he attended eighteen-year-old Dessie's wedding. What a surprising moment for me.

My grandmother had been the first recipient of the loving care the Shakes had poured out and Roy had carried forward in his life. My grandmother recovered from the deep and abiding losses of her childhood as she came to know Jesus in the Shakes' small church in Illinois and as she experienced the unconditional love of that amazing couple who cared for her in those devastating years after the death of her

---

[2]Thema Bryant-Davis, Monica U. Ellis, Elizabeth Burke-Maynard, Nathan Moon, Pamela A. Counts, and Gera Anderson, "Religiosity, Spirituality, and Trauma Recovery in the Lives of Children and Adolescents," *Professional Psychology: Research and Practice* 43, no. 4 (2012): 306-14.

mother, brother, and father. Her resilience is her tangible legacy. My grandmother poured that same love for Jesus and his Word, along with unconditional love and support, over many children in her rural community . . . and over me.

THIS AUDACIOUS TASK

Telling stories of resilience and telling Bible stories in a way that nurtures children's relationships with God, self, and others can help children enter God's master story. These stories allow children to see God's work in the world not only in centuries gone by but also in recent years and even now. Creating ways to enter God's story with children is a challenging task for Sunday school teachers. Sunday schools need not do everything to nurture children spiritually; parents as well as the whole body of Christ are also called to this task. However, for most children, Sunday school is the only place where they systematically learn God's story and their place in it. The child-God relationship cannot flourish unless children know this God, who he is, what God has been doing in the world, how they are called into this story, and what God is doing in them as they enter his story.

Furthermore, it is in this space that children become more grounded in their identity as children of God and begin to absorb a deep sense of belonging—both of which are key resilience qualities.

CHAPTER EIGHT

Body and Spirit

THADDEUS, A LIPSCOMB UNIVERSITY STUDENT who was taking my Nurturing Children's Spirituality course, functioned as Tyrone's mentor for ten weeks. Tyrone had been raised by his single mom along with some aunts and uncles. His biological dad was in his life, but he lived some distance away. In one of their mentoring meetings, the Lipscomb students and their mentees walked a labyrinth together in pairs. When Tyrone's turn came, he was distracted by the interesting design of the labyrinth, the electric candles at the entrance and in the center, and the process of walking to the center and back out again. Thaddeus said Tyrone didn't seem to attend to the quiet process and appeared to be somewhat overwhelmed.

A few weeks later Thaddeus and Tyrone had another opportunity to walk the labyrinth. In his final journal entry for the course, Thaddeus reported:

> This time was different. This time, Tyrone led us in. He was some distance ahead of me and got to the center quickly. When we reached the center, he pulled out a set of prayer beads we had assembled a couple of weeks earlier. At that time, I had shown him how to move the beads down the string, praying, then to move the beads back, listening. In the center of the labyrinth, Tyrone began to move the beads. I was surprised at the slow pace he set; he was very intentional, spending more time as he prayed.

Parts of this chapter were adapted from Holly Catterton Allen, "Body and Spirit: The Role of Physical Movement in Children's Spiritual Development" (with John Brown University students Robin Howerton, Will Chesher, and Hannah Brown), in *Exploring and Engaging Spirituality for Today's Children: A Holistic Approach*, ed. La Verne Tolbert (Eugene, OR: Wipf & Stock, 2014), 195-209. Used by permission of Wipf and Stock Publishers, www.wipfandstock.com.

After he moved the last bead back, I asked him what he prayed for. "My family," he said, and proceeded to tell who each bead was and how he had prayed for them.

I began to see something important I had not noticed before. Typically, when Tyrone mentioned his family, he talked about his mom; however, when Tyrone had drawn his family on the first day we had met, he had started with his aunt and uncle, adding another uncle, a grandmother, and three other aunts. I realized in that moment in the center of the labyrinth with the beads how important Tyrone's extended family is to him; he revealed this to me in this body-spirit activity. In our remaining weeks, we spoke often of those empowering aunts and uncles in his life.[1]

BODY, MIND, AND SPIRIT?

Those who teach children in any setting have been intentionally incorporating bodily movement for decades. They use movement to get the wiggles out, to illustrate a song, to transition to another activity or change the pace, or to act out a story. Besides knowing that movement makes learning more fun, these teachers are also aware that educational specialists recommend movement to enhance learning—that is, they know that a strong body-mind connection exists.

But this chapter goes beyond the body-mind connection to explore the body-spirit relationship. The body-spirit connection has been neglected due in part to the sometimes negative view of the physical body in the history of Western Christianity. That is, the body has commonly been perceived as a liability in spiritual formation rather than as an asset. This chapter seeks to illustrate how the body can contribute positively to the spiritual growth and development of children[2] and ultimately to resilience in children as well.

A body-spirit disconnect. Christians have tended toward a mixed theology regarding the relationship of body and spirit. One early source of this mixed theology is Plato's dualistic view of human nature that has

---

[1] Used with permission of Thaddeus Billingsley.
[2] The key insights from this chapter apply not only to children and their spirituality, but to adults and their spiritual lives as well.

influenced Western thinking about spirituality for millennia.[3] Though Plato is not uniformly dualistic in his writings, in general he considered life to be a battle between the bodily passions that drag us down and the rational/spiritual essence that can discern truth, beauty, and reality. Centuries later Augustine in some of his writings described the body as a weapon of sin and man as a soul "using" a body; his comments regarding sexual intercourse between a husband and wife as sinful except for the purpose of progeny[4] have especially contributed to the general body-spirit disconnect that emerged in early Christianity.

Although monks carried forward the Christian faith in many good ways through the medieval period, some pursued spirituality to the detriment of the body, for example, fasting to sickness or death, living in solitary confinement, going without sleep, and exposing themselves to the elements. These examples reflect the notion of body as a barrier rather than a benefit to spirituality.

This body-spirit dissonance has wafted down through Christianity and perhaps still tends to negatively influence believers' views of the role of the body in spiritual formation. However, Christians should have a high theology of the physical body in light of the fact that God became human in the form of Jesus.[5] And Scripture offers numerous examples of embodied spirituality. Below is a partial listing:

- Exodus 15:20: Miriam and the other women dancing after being delivered from Egypt.
- Deuteronomy 26:10: "'Bring the firstfruits. . . . ' Place the basket before the LORD your God and bow down before him."
- 2 Samuel 6:14: "David was dancing before the LORD with all his might."
- Psalm 30:11: "You turned my wailing into dancing; you removed my sackcloth and clothed me with joy."

[3]Mike Radford, "Spirituality and Education: Inner and Outer Realities." *International Journal of Children's Spirituality* 11, no. 3 (2006): 385-96.

[4]Augustine, *Soliloquies: Augustine's Inner Dialogue* (Hyde Park, NY: New City Press, 2000).

[5]Thomas Ryan, "Toward a Positive Spirituality of the Body," in *Reclaiming the Body in Christian Spirituality,* ed. Thomas Ryan (Mahwah, NJ: Paulist Press, 2004).

- Psalm 47:1: "Clap your hands, all you nations; shout to God with cries of joy."
- Psalm 95:6: "Come, let us bow down in worship, let us kneel before the Lord our Maker."
- Luke 7:38: The woman who washed Jesus' feet with her tears and anointed them with ointment.
- John 13:5-14: Jesus washing the disciples' feet; the disciples washing one another's feet.
- Acts 2:2-4: The Holy Spirit enabling those in the upper room to speak in other languages.
- Acts 2:38: "Repent and be baptized."
- Romans 16:16: "Greet one another with a holy kiss."
- 1 Corinthians 6:15, 20: "Do you not know that your bodies are members of Christ himself? . . . Therefore honor God with your bodies."
- 1 Corinthians 11:23-26: "For I received from the Lord what I also passed on to you: The Lord Jesus, on the night he was betrayed, took bread, and when he had given thanks, he broke it and said, 'This is my body, which is for you; do this in remembrance of me.' In the same way, after supper he took the cup, saying, 'This cup is the new covenant in my blood; do this, whenever you drink it, in remembrance of me.' For whenever you eat this bread and drink this cup, you proclaim the Lord's death until he comes."
- 1 Timothy 2:8: "Therefore I want the men everywhere to pray, lifting up holy hands without anger or disputing."
- James 5:14: "Is anyone among you sick? Let them call the elders of the church to pray over them and anoint them with oil in the name of the Lord."

Though some in Christian history have minimized, overlooked, or even denounced employing the body to promote spiritual formation, others have recognized that the body can contribute positively to spirituality. God's people have been known to "bow, sing, anoint with oil, greet with a kiss of peace, go on nature retreats, teach children to kneel for bedtime prayers, make the sign of the cross, shake hands, act out passion plays, prostrate themselves, applaud, participate in ropes courses, dance, lay hands on a person, stand, speak in tongues, kneel, close eyes, walk labyrinths, twirl, dress modestly, put motions to lyrics, shout, raise hands, wash feet, bow heads, cry, fold hands, play instruments, fast, feast, slay in the Spirit, baptize, read responsively, dedicate babies, lament, welcome new believers, and take communion, to list many common physical practices with spiritual intentions."[6] Clearly, believers through the ages have combined the spiritual and the physical in numerous ways.

And recent findings in the hard sciences are currently contributing to our understanding of mind-body-spirit connections. Andrew Newberg, a neurotheologian, conducted experiments for a couple of decades that examined what is going on in the brain when participants are engaged in meditation, speaking in tongues, centered prayer, and other spiritual-physical activities.[7]

In the years since his first experiments with nuns and monks,[8] Newberg has come to believe that our brains are wired for belief. He summarizes his understanding of the brain and religious-spiritual interconnectedness, saying, "What fires together, wires together"—that is, "The more [one uses] a particular pathway of neurons, the more

---

[6]Allen, "Body and Spirit," 200. Robbie Howerton, one of my former students at John Brown University, originally gathered this wonderful descriptive list for a paper in the course Nurturing Spiritual Development in Children.

[7]Andrew Newberg and Stephanie Newberg, "A Neuropsychological Perspective on Spiritual Development," in *Handbook of Spiritual Development in Childhood and Adolescence,* ed. Peter Benson, Eugene Roehlkepartain, Pamela King, and Linda Wagener (London: Sage Publications, 2005), 183-96; Eugene G. d'Aquili and Andrew B. Newberg, "Religious and Mystical States: A Neuropsychological Model," *Zygon* 28 (1993): 177-200.

[8]Newberg's best-known brain-imaging experiments were performed with Tibetan Buddhist monks, Franciscan nuns, and Pentecostals. Newberg and his team first injected radioactive material into participants' brains, then took neural snapshots of the brains—first at a base level when participants were not involved in any type of religious activity, then another photo during the peak of their religious activity; for Buddhist monks, it was the peak of meditation (as indicated by the participant); for Franciscan nuns it was during a centering prayer; and, for Pentecostals, while they were speaking in tongues. The second photos revealed a decrease in activity in the parietal lobe, which is the orienting part of the brain; this decrease in activity is associated with somebody losing a "sense of self," which the participants described as spiritually transcendent (Andrew Newberg, "Neuroscience and Religion: Neuroepistemology," in *Encyclopedia of Religion,* 2nd ed., vol 10, ed. Lindsay Jones [Farmington Hills, MI: Thompson Gale, 2005]).

strongly they become connected to each other."[9] Newberg says regularly worshiping at a church or synagogue, hearing the same stories, saying certain prayers, and participating in the same rituals stimulate and strengthen neural pathways. As these physical religious experiences create connections to the spiritual—these neural pathways are fortified. Newberg's neurotheological work helps us see how body, brain, and spirit are integrally interconnected.

CONNECTING CHILDREN'S SPIRITUALITY WITH THE BODY

Much of the rest of this chapter will describe ways to employ the body to enhance spiritual formation. What can be done in the body that can especially nurture children (and others) spiritually?

Prayer and the body. A few years ago, when I was addressing a large audience, a sign language interpreter was translating for several participants who were hard of hearing. As I opened the session with prayer, I cast my eyes over all who were gathered; I was fascinated by the sign linguist as she captured the words of the prayer in visual representation. Later I asked her if she would teach all the participants the signs for a few words. The prayer we would be praying together was: "Lord, you are holy; God, we give you glory."

The interpreter taught us the hand signs for "Lord," "holy," "God," and "glory." The signs for "holy" and "glory" are beautiful and expressive; the signs for "Lord" and "God" embody reverence and exalt God as Sovereign Lord. As the group prayed and signed, "Lord, you are holy; God, we give you glory," I watched a thousand people bestow honor on their Lord with their hearts, souls, and *bodies*. It was an inspiring, touching moment.

Doug Pagitt and Kathryn Prill are also keenly aware of this body-spirit prayer connection. In their book *Body Prayer: The Posture of Intimacy*

---

[9]Andrew Newberg, "How Our Brains Are Wired for Belief" (presentation, Faith Angle Conference, Key West, FL, May 5, 2008), www.pewforum.org/2008/05/05/how-our-brains-are-wired-for-belief; Andrew Newberg, "Transformation of Brain Structure and Spiritual Experience," in *The Oxford Handbook of Psychology and Spirituality,* ed. Lisa Miller (Oxford, UK: Oxford University Press, 2012), 489-99.

with God, they have written thirty prayers, offering accompanying bodily position or actions for each prayer to reflect and help create prayerful attitudes. For example, here is their prayer of enjoyment:

> May the Lord be praised
> From now and evermore.
> We are blessed by his redemption
> And filled with his love.
> May the Lord be praised
> From now and evermore.[10]

The body posture description reads simply, "Standing, clasp your hands by interlocking your fingers, then stretch your arms over your head."[11] The postures are really physical reflections of spiritual postures. The spiritual and physical are connected, influencing each other in these postural movements. Children enjoy enacting these prayers and, of course, love creating their own bodily motions for prayers, teaching other children, and explaining why they chose specific movements.

Thus far we have discussed adding specific bodily movements to prayer. Another way to consider the body-spirit connection is to add prayer to common physical activities such as chores, getting dressed for the day, or preparing for bedtime. Some of the prayers that have been preserved from the days of Celtic Christianity reflect this body-spirit relationship; for example, the following prayer was recited while milking the cow:

> Bless, O God, my desire;
> Bless thou my partnership
> And the milking of my hands, O God.[12]

For children today, making their bed offers an opportunity for a specific prayer; unloading the dishwasher, taking out the trash, vacuuming, dusting, putting away toys, brushing teeth, or taking a bath are others. Helping children create short prayers that accompany such mundane tasks can transport these ordinary physical activities into the spiritual realm.

---

[10]Doug Pagitt and Kathryn Prill, *Body Prayer: The Posture of Intimacy with God* (Colorado Springs, CO: Random House, 2005), 24.

[11]Pagitt and Prill, *Body Prayer,* 24.

[12]Tracy Balzer, *Thin Places: An Evangelical Journey into Celtic Christianity* (Abilene, TX: Leafwood, 2007), 77.

Dance. Dance is a biblical form of worship. Psalm 149:3 says, "Let them praise his name with dancing," and Psalm 150:4 says, "Praise him with timbrel and dancing." King David not only recommended dancing as a way to worship God, but he also practiced what he preached: "As the ark of the covenant of the LORD was entering the City of David, Michal daughter of Saul . . . saw King David dancing" (1 Chronicles 15:29).

Worshipers in most faith traditions in Western Christianity don't tend to dance (though in charismatic churches it is typically more acceptable). The church has been uneasy about including dance in worship due to the dualism that has equated the spirit with good and the body with evil[13] as has been noted earlier in this chapter.

Children, music, and dance fit wonderfully together. Young children typically are very comfortable expressing their spirituality through dance and other bodily movement as they experience joy, sadness, wonder—even dealing with suffering and questioning meaning.[14] Thus, those of us who work with children may wish to create opportunities for children, especially young children, to dance in response to God's work in the world.

One of the most profound and memorable moments of my life happened at the 2006 Children's Spirituality Conference held at Concordia University in River Forest, Illinois. Ten children enacted through dance six verses and the refrain of Chris Rice's song "Come to Jesus." The verses follow the life journey of one coming to Jesus, hitting hard places, rejoicing in the good times, and eventually facing the journey's end.

As I watched that evening, the children . . .

- bowed low in hopelessness,
- reached for Jesus,
- rejoiced in finding him,
- bowed low again in loneliness and pain,
- spread their hands over their heads to protect themselves,

---

[13]Robert E. Webber, *Music and the Arts in Christian Worship* (Book 2), *The Complete Library of Christian Worship: Vol. 4B* ed. by Robert E. Webber (Nashville: Star Song Publishing Group, 1994).

[14]Carolyn R. Muller, "Spirituality in Children: Understanding and Developing Interventions," *Pediatric Nursing* 36, no. 4 (2010): 197-208.

- laced themselves together to catch one falling,
- danced delightfully with joy, and
- exited the stage, "flying" to Jesus.

Even now as I recall those lyrical moments, my eyes fill at this remembered display of body-spirit connection. As much as this moment affected me, I believe its effect on the children was even more profound. They interpreted and enacted those meaningful words as one who is lost, found, wounded, held, and received. Each child expressed the meaning of the words in his or her body—the child-self connection; the ten children worked in pairs and as a group to express the complex relational aspects of the words—the child-others connection; and every verse explicitly drew them to Jesus—the child-God connection.

Perhaps more than any other suggestion in this chapter, the movement of dance connects in unique ways with children and can be a conduit between the child and the self, others, and God.

Labyrinths. One fascinating way to combine movement with quietness is by walking a labyrinth, as Tyrone discovered during his mentoring sessions with Thaddeus.

European Christians in the Middle Ages would sometimes make pilgrimages to the Holy Land. The pilgrims would prepare for the dangerous and expensive trip possibly for years. The process was viewed as a three-part journey: (1) releasing one of family, work, and life responsibilities as one made the long journey to Jerusalem, (2) entering the place of Jesus' earthly existence, walking where he walked, dwelling in a sense in his presence, and then (3) returning: making the long trip home where one would once again take up one's former responsibilities in life.

Because the trip was so costly and long, few could make it. It is thought that labyrinths were created so that more "pilgrims" could participate in a representation of the journey. The most famous labyrinth was incorporated into Chartres Cathedral in France built in the 1200s. A person can simulate the trip to the Holy Land by walking the labyrinth: (1) releasing responsibilities as one walks toward the center, (2) "entering" into a sacred space (dwelling in the center of the labyrinth that represents Christ), and then (3) returning to one's responsibilities, walking out of the labyrinth.

Walking a labyrinth today can represent just such a journey. I have created labyrinths many times, most often in a large cleared room utilizing masking tape on the floor, or using desks, chairs, or other furniture to form the labyrinth. A room full of folding chairs in rows adapts quite easily. Or one can spray-paint a labyrinth design outside in a large patch of grass. Two years ago, I fashioned a portable labyrinth by painting the design in black enamel on a fifteen-by-fifteen-foot canvas drop cloth.

Most labyrinths are designed as unguided personal experiences, as aids for individuals to:

- Release burdens and leave anxiety behind as they enter.
- Walk circuitously to the center where they rest, wait, and dwell while quietly receiving from Christ.
- Slowly move back through the labyrinth toward the opening, returning to their ordinary lives refreshed and renewed.

Children especially enjoy walking labyrinths since they offer a unique and fascinating venue to combine the spiritual with bodily movement. Labyrinths seem perfectly designed to open a space for wounded children to listen, process their losses, and hear from God.

CONNECTING EMBODIED SPIRITUALITY AND RESILIENCE

For children, engaging the spiritual realm through the body is natural. Rather than hindering children in their bodily expression, those of us who work with children should perhaps be more intentional in nurturing the body-spirit connection by incorporating physical practices with spiritual intentions such as walking a labyrinth, utilizing prayer beads, creating opportunities for dance, and providing sacred space and times of quiet and stillness. As we do so, children who are grappling with troubling experiences will lean into the God who knows and loves them, connect with others in deeper ways, and come to know themselves better, intersecting especially with such resilience qualities as self-awareness and self-efficacy.

Consider the story of Autumn and her seven-year-old mentee, Lucy. Lucy came to the mentoring meetings with a take-charge attitude. She seemed to need to be in control, typically rejecting whatever activity was planned for the day. Autumn caught on quickly that it was important for Lucy to come to the planned activity by choice, and she creatively orchestrated processes whereby that could happen. Lucy also resisted self-revelatory opportunities, preferring to give "churchy" answers and surface responses. Over the weeks Autumn was able to discern a couple of issues Lucy was coping with, including her adoptive status and some relationships with school friends. But the elephant in the room, which Lucy did not address, was that her mother had been diagnosed about a year earlier with an aggressive, terminal cancer. Lucy studiously avoided any reference to that subject.

Near the end of the semester, Lucy and Autumn walked the labyrinth together. Lucy initially ignored the guidelines: rather than following her mentor, she jumped ahead; rather than walking slowly, she ran around the labyrinth, stepping across lines; rather than waiting for her mentor to light the candle, she clicked on the electric candle as soon as she reached the center. When Autumn reached the center, she expected Lucy to ignore the guidelines there as well (sit quietly, talk to God, wait, listen to God), but Lucy did in fact sit quietly in the center, bowing her head, sitting there for several minutes until Autumn eventually called her back to the moment. Lucy looked up and, with tears in her eyes, asked, "What will I do without my mama?" When Autumn tentatively reached for Lucy's hand, Lucy clung to it tightly as her tears fell.

This quiet moment, this physical opportunity to traverse a labyrinth, sit in a special place, and intentionally listen, had connected with Lucy as nothing else had that semester. She was able to finally ask the only question in her mind: What would she do without her mother?

This story has a postscript. A few months later I invited the students from one of my classes to our home for dinner and to make homemade doughnuts; I also invited the family down the street to join us—Lucy's family. This family had been in our home a few other times, but this time I specifically invited them because Autumn would be there and she and Lucy would have an opportunity to see each other again.

Neither Autumn nor I expected what happened when Lucy came in the door. When she spotted Autumn, she ran to her, put her arms around her waist, and gently leaned her head against Autumn, eyes closed. All evening, when not eating or glazing doughnuts, Lucy sat on Autumn's lap, restful and at peace. The only time during the previous semester that Lucy had let down her guard was in the center of the labyrinth, so Autumn had not known that Lucy saw her as a safe, caring person. It was a tender, poignant moment for Autumn and me, but most importantly for Lucy, who was still asking the question, "What will I do without my mother?"

CONCLUSION

These stories indicate to me that engaging children bodily can create a conduit to their inner being, perhaps in ways that other processes cannot.

In ways we don't fully understand, the physical and spiritual are inseparable. All of our interactions with God are simply, by default, experienced by the whole person.[15] According to Eugene Peterson, "The body is not a barrier to spirituality; indeed, it is the only access we have."[16] These statements, though perhaps originally meant for adults, are no less true for children. Perhaps they are even more true for children, since children seem to comprehend instinctively that the physical and the spiritual are integrally connected. Generally, they are more in tune with their bodies than adults and are typically less inhibited.[17]

Children begin life with a sense of the inexpressible mystery of God. As adults, we are called by God to nurture that sense of the holy in children. It is an audacious task—to help children seek the ineffable— and creating opportunities that integrate the physical and spiritual is a surprisingly powerful way to nurture the child-self, child-others, and child-God relationships and along the way contribute to their resilience.

---

[15]Darrel Cox, "The Physical Body in Spiritual Formation: What God Has Joined Together Let No One Put Asunder," *Journal of Psychology and Christianity* 21, no. 3 (2002).

[16]Eugene Peterson, "St. Mark: The Basic Text for Christian Spirituality" (keynote address, North American Professors of Christian Education Conference, Seattle, WA, October 20, 2011).

[17]Thomas W. Moore, "Transpersonal Education: A Preview," *Journal of Education* 157, no. 4 (1975): 24-39.

CHAPTER NINE

Wonder

AROUND THE AGE OF FOUR many children go through an exhausting "why" phase:

- Why does Daddy have big hairs in his nose?
- Why do people sneeze?
- Why do people have two eyes and two ears and only one nose?
- Why do dogs have to die?
- Why do people have to die?
- Why doesn't God just fix it?

Some children never grow out of this stage, asking ever-more-complex questions about life, humankind, the universe, and God. David, the psalmist, asks:

> When I consider your heavens,
>   the work of your fingers,
> the moon and the stars,
>   which you have set in place,
> what is mankind that you are mindful of them,
>   human beings that you care for them? (Psalm 8:3-4)

David spent his youth shepherding his family's flocks; he was out in the cold, the damp, the heat, the storm. He had the time to contemplate the heavens and the God of Abraham, Isaac, and Jacob, to wonder about who human beings are and who God is.

Many children drop the "why" questions as the trappings of school and life overtake them. As Richard Winter says, "The media have so constantly bombarded us with the stimulating and spectacular that our sense of wonder in the life and the world that God has given us has atrophied."[1] One of the most important things we can do for our children to nurture them spiritually is to ensure that they have time and space to see, to listen, to hear—that is, the time and space to *be*.

Sadly, adults are sometimes to blame for depriving children of the time and space to simply be, as we tend to provide constant entertainment, excitement, and novelty.[2] Even in our Sunday school classrooms and our children's church settings, we have sometimes lost the deeper purpose of our teaching when we have focused on entertaining, exciting, and novel ways in our efforts to be developmentally appropriate.

Once I was asked to observe the preschool and kindergarten Sunday school classes in a large church to offer insight and input. During the first kindergarten class I observed, the Bible story focused on Lydia, the Christ-follower in Acts who was a seller of purple. The class opened with a fabulous painting opportunity; buckets of blue and red paint were set around the room and the walls were covered with white butcher paper and the floors with large sheaths of clear plastic covering. The aproned children were given paintbrushes to dip in the blue, then the red paint and see what happened when they painted the wall. Of course, fabulous purples, lilacs, violets, magentas, and aubergines bloomed around the room. This activity took about twenty to twenty-five minutes, then the children gathered round for the telling of the story, which lasted about six minutes. Next, some delicious purple cupcakes appeared and were devoured straightaway. For the last ten minutes of class, several satin, sequined, silky drapes of purple cloth were distributed around the room for a few moments of dress-up. The children and the teachers really enjoyed the class; however, I found myself wondering if the ubiquitous kindergarten developmental objective of color knowledge may have hijacked the day.

Perhaps the teachers could have walked around the room and gently asked some of the following preschool-level wondering questions: Why

---

[1]Richard Winter, *Still Bored in a Culture of Entertainment: Rediscovering Passion and Wonder* (Downers Grove, IL: InterVarsity Press, 2002), 117.
[2]Winter, *Still Bored.*

do you suppose God made the color purple? Where in this world do we see purple? Is purple important? Why? Why do we have so many colors? What would the world be like without color? Why do you think God made colors? Even though these questions are still focused on the color purple, they can transport the wonderful painting, eating, and dress-up experiences into a deeper realm.

Another week when I visited, the story of David and Goliath was told. The focus that day was the number five, another developmentally appropriate kindergarten goal: everyone ate five crackers, counted five stones, colored five stones, found five stones hidden in the room. Last, the children threw five (papier-mâché) stones at a nine-foot cardboard Goliath. The teachers kept them busy, interested, going from center to center, occupied. Again, the children enjoyed the class, and they probably learned the number five, but were they given an opportunity to consider David's faith in God? Did they hear David's testimony, "The LORD who rescued me from the paw of the lion and the paw of the bear will rescue me from the hand of this Philistine" (1 Samuel 17:37)? Was there time and space for these five-year-olds to wonder about how David learned to trust in God?

In one of his more philosophical writings, Jerome Berryman (creator of Godly Play) discusses three ways of knowing:

• The knowing of the material world by the senses
• The knowing of the mind by using reason
• The knowing of the spirit by contemplation[3]

Berryman says our body-knowing and our spirit-knowing develop first (since the mind-knowing needs language to flourish). Because children are spiritual beings, they begin early to intuit spiritual knowing through contemplation, but spirit-knowing is sometimes lost in typical school settings where body-knowing and mind-knowing are often more valued. When we overlook the spirit-knowing with children in our classrooms, counseling sessions, or in our homes, we hinder their spiritual potential.[4] All three kinds of knowing are a valuable part of religious

---

[3]Jerome W. Berryman, "Spirituality, Religious Education, and the Dormouse," *International Journal of Children's Spirituality* 2, no. 1 (1997): 9-23.
[4]Berryman, "Spirituality, Religious Education, and the Dormouse."

education, Berryman says, but he posits that Christian educators may have neglected the knowing of the spirit through contemplation, and this is the kind of knowing that requires wondering. We need to allow time for this spiritual knowing—allowing time for children to think, listen, perceive, receive. Do we leave time for children to experience the wonder of God? What might this look like?

STORYTELLING AND WONDER

One of the goals of storytelling is to engage wonder.[5] One of the best ways for children to enter stories is to have the opportunity to re-create them. For young children, acting out the story works very well. However, reenacting the story is not the end—it is merely a means for helping children enter the story and to help them wonder. Afterward, asking each child who played a role to express his or her feelings about being Deborah, King Saul, Jairus, or Miriam can help children enter the wondering place. Following this discussion with the question, "I wonder what God was doing in this story?" can help children orient toward a God who is at work in the world.

Asking middle-to-older elementary children to write the background story for children (or others) in the Bible can facilitate their entering the wondering place as well. Examples of "expanding the story" prompts could include:

- Create a fuller story around the life of the slave girl whom Naaman's armies took captive (2 Kings 5).
- Describe the life and times of Jairus's daughter, her relationship with her dad, and the trust she had in him to find Jesus to save her (Mark 5).
- Chronicle a day in the life of Josiah in the first year of his reign when he was eight years old (2 Chronicles 34–35).

When the children share their imaginings of these stories, ask, "I wonder how Naaman's slave/Jairus's daughter/Josiah learned to trust God?" This process can lead to other wondering questions regarding their own rela-

---

[5]Jerome W. Berryman, *Godly Play: A Way of Religious Education* (HarperSanFrancisco, 1991).

tionship with God, such as, "I wonder how you are learning to trust God?"

STILLNESS AND SILENCE

Another spiritual and physical behavior we can employ with children to nurture their spiritual development is stillness. Often teachers are encouraged to use physical movement, activity, and busyness to engage children, and indeed, physical movement typically does engage children. However, creating opportunities for stillness, places for meditation, and venues for listening to God can offer an alternative and unusual (for children) approach to wonder. Those who write about spiritual disciplines for adults describe multiple ways to be still before God (e.g., journaling, lectio divina, silent retreats, meditation); however, we seldom employ these "adult" spiritual strategies with children, perhaps because we doubt the ability of children to be still or to hear from God.

But children need space, just as adults do, to discern the work of God in them; parents and teachers can create "sacred space—a space laden with expectation, transcendence, and mystery," according to Myers.[6]

One semester the children who were part of our spiritual development course mentioned earlier were brought to Lipscomb's campus on Saturdays to meet with their mentors. Lipscomb student Jessica reported that her mentee, Cici, initially seemed tentative when they discussed God. During the first couple of weeks the children and mentors were together, they read children's books together and drew pictures—safe, comfortable activities. Sometimes they sat in the campus swings talking or listening to the birds and the fountain, occasionally working through a few questions about God. Jessica reported that Cici hesitated before responding to some of the questions, and she shared no church experiences during their conversations. Jessica gathered from these observations that Cici's background included few formal faith experiences. In her final report, Jessica wrote, "It was quite touching on our last Saturday, that after we came out of the school cafeteria, [Cici] saw a swing on the

[6]Barbara Kimes Myers, *Young Children and Spirituality* (New York: Routledge, 1997), 78.

campus, and she looked up at me and eagerly asked, 'Are we going to sit in the swing and talk about God?'"

Those quiet, unhurried moments of sitting in the swings talking about God had been special times for Cici, though Jessica had not realized it until the end of their weeks together.

Children may need help to quiet not only their bodies but also their hearts. In general, most church programs for children have not allowed much space for stillness and contemplation; typically, few opportunities are provided for children to wonder about themselves or about God. Berryman poses this question: "What if the origins of the religious life and the special language for expressing and exploring the spiritual quest are to be found precisely in silence?"[7]

Godly Play is a contemplative-reflective approach to teaching that can help children learn to quiet themselves.[8] Bible stories are told with softened voice and specially textured support materials, and after each story several wondering questions are asked. Most of these questions are designed not to elicit discussion but to provide opportunity for children to wonder internally—for example, "I wonder where this place could really be?" or "I wonder which part is most important?" Godly Play taps into the unique body-spirit process of stillness; in the quietness that follows the wondering questions, children often sit in silence, considering, listening. According to Sofia Cavalletti, posing questions without answering them helps the child to meditate on the story.[9]

After the storytelling time in Godly Play, children are allowed to choose a story that has been told previously and play with the special pieces that tell the story. Often when children do this, they can be overheard asking the very wondering questions the leader asked earlier: "Who do you think could be the neighbor of the priest?" "Who do you think could be the neighbor of the robber?" Sometimes children will offer commentary on the characters in the story: "You're a church man!

---

[7]Berryman, 1991, *Godly Play,* 140.
[8]Jerome W. Berryman, *Teaching Godly Play: The Sunday Morning Handbook* (Denver: Morehouse Education Resources, 2009).
[9]Sofia Cavalletti, *The Religious Potential of the Child* (New York: Paulist Press, 1983), 66.

How come you didn't help that man who got robbed?" Or "I bet you knew the Good Shepherd was going to come back for you, didn't you?" In their commentary, it can be seen that the children were entering the story, identifying with some of the characters, questioning others.

Stewart and Berryman summarize the role of wondering in these contemplative storytelling moments:

> The time for wondering is a time of reflection, when a group engages in an open shared dialogue with the story, with one another, and with their experiences in the story. Wondering together . . . shapes and deepens our knowledge of God and what God expects of us. It is a way the community of children comes to know God and themselves. This knowing is based on their experience of God, not on being told about God. Their experience of God in the story informs their expression, and their expression, refined by the group, begins to name their world.[10]

Godly Play is one way to incorporate wondering questions into our teaching time with children, but there are other ways as well. In almost every Bible story we tell, there is a place to insert some imagining moments:

- In the story of Esther, after Mordecai encouraged Esther to go to the king, there followed a period of three days of fasting and prayer. The children can imagine what Esther was saying to God and what God might have been saying to Esther.
- In Joseph's story, during the moments when he was in the pit, consider what Joseph was saying to God and what God was saying to Joseph.
- In the story of the feeding of the five thousand, imagine what the little boy may have been thinking before he shared his lunch, what he might have been saying to God, and what God may have been saying to him.

After any teaching time, you can open space for wonder by saying, "Close your eyes. Imagine you were in this story. Who were you? How did you feel? What did you see?"[11] Or you can offer some time to draw, asking

---

[10]Sonja M. Stewart and Jerome Berryman, *Young Children and Worship* (Louisville, KY: Westminster John Knox Press, 1989), 30.
[11]This approach is based around the Ignatian practice of imaginative prayer. See Kevin O'Brien, SJ,

children to sketch something they saw during the previous week that was simply beautiful. In the quiet that follows, God can reveal himself and the beauty he creates.

Leaving open space—creating sacred space—in our time with children allows them to think, listen, perceive—and to ask, "Who are you, Lord?"[12]

THE CHILD-WORLD RELATIONSHIP

This is a good place to share a bit about the child-world relationship that is mentioned in two spirituality definitions I referenced briefly in chapter one. Abiding in nature is a spiritual language for some children. Playing outside nurtures and fills them. For some, it is a channel to God.

One summer night in the Davis Mountains in Southwest Texas far from city lights, near the McDonald Observatory, my family stood beneath some of the darkest and clearest night skies in the United States and beheld a most amazing panoply of stars. Our children were seven, nine, and fifteen when we witnessed this astonishing display, and it remains a spiritual marker for our family.

Jill grew up in a home where anger ruled and soul-crushing negativity reigned. Behind her home, a tree-lined creek wound its way through her neighborhood. On summer days throughout her childhood, Jill would make her way to a bend in the creek where the small stream pooled; a tree had fallen across this diminutive pond making a private oasis for solitude in God's verdant creation. In this place, Jill read, thought, and considered God. God met her there, received her, welcomed her, and comforted her—before she was aware that comfort was what she needed. This place was a safe space for her, a place where God came near.

Other children find their oasis perched high in a tree, riding their bikes, growing flowers, fishing, or hiking in state parks. All of these can be places of wonder, where children's souls are filled and fortified for the days to come.

Tennessee Prison Outreach Ministry in Nashville offers a summer

---

The Ignatian Adventure: Experiencing the Spiritual Exercises of St. Ignatius in Daily Life (Chicago: Loyola Press, 2011).

[12]Cavalletti, *The Religious Potential of the Child.*

camp for children whose parents are incarcerated. The children who attend get to canoe, swim, hike, play group games, and sit outside and just *be*. They can watch the sun rise and the sun set listening for God's presence in their lives. Some of these children do not have safe outdoor spaces where they live. This summer camp offers space to listen, to heal, to participate in the beauty of the world, and to wonder.

This place is called Camp Cope.

CHILDREN'S SPIRITUALITY, WONDER, AND RESILIENCE

This chapter has explored ways to create contexts for children to experience wonder while they are alone as well as when they are with others. It discusses how posing questions without answering them helps the child enter a story and how wondering together is a community's way of remaining open to the Holy Spirit, a way of meditating so the story becomes a part of the group's life. Wondering shapes and deepens our knowledge of God.[13] As Borgo says, "When children are invited to listen and look for the movement of God in their life, it is a tangible reminder that they are not alone and opens them to the possibility of resiliency when life feels overwhelming."[14]

All of my observation and ministry experience confirms for me that God initiates spiritual relationship with children, and children respond to his invitation. Those around the child can ignore, dampen, or discourage that response, or they can recognize, encourage, and nurture the spiritual response in children. We want to create communities where children see God at work, experience God, and come to know God with others who are also coming to know God. As children's spirituality (particularly their relationship with God) is nurtured and encouraged, the children will be equipped to endure the adversities that will come their way. They will be more equipped to face with fortitude hardship, loss, or grief as they engage with a God they have come to know in moments of quiet and wonder.

---

[13]Stewart and Berryman, *Young Children and Worship*.

[14]Lacy Finn Borgo, *Spiritual Conversations with Children* (Downers Grove, IL: InterVarsity Press, 2020), 43.

PART FOUR

Children's Spirituality, Resilience, and Adversity

CHAPTER TEN

Severe Trauma

MY FIRST TEACHING POSITION was at a rural school in Mississippi, where I taught fifth grade. Twelve-year-old Reba and her sister Pam, eleven, were both in my fifth grade homeroom. On the first Monday in November that fall, Reba and Pam came to school in bandages.

Over the weekend their family had engaged in a gunfight in which Reba was grazed across the forehead and Pam's elbow was shot. On Monday, Reba's head was bandaged heavily and Pam's arm was in a sling. I couldn't imagine what could happen in a family where the children would be shot.

Two years later, I was teaching second grade in a large school in the Whitehaven area of Memphis, Tennessee. I received a new student in early January whose name was Rose. No test scores or other school records were passed on to me, so I placed Rose in the middle reading group until I could discern where she might fit.

For the first two days Rose did not speak; she said not a word to me or the other students, though she would nod her head yes or no in response to questions. I was unsure how to proceed, so I made an appointment with the school counselor. I told the counselor about Rose's behavior, and she explained that Rose's stepfather had sexually abused her, that she was now living in a foster home, and that she was in counseling. She had no other words of wisdom for me.

Parts of this chapter were adapted from Holly Catterton Allen, "Resilience, Trauma, and Children's Spirituality" (with Lipscomb students Kaylee Frank and Megan Larry), in *Bridging Theory and Practice in Children's Spirituality,* ed. Mimi Larson and Robert Keeley (Grand Rapids, MI: Zondervan, 2020). Used by permission of Zondervan, www.zondervan.com.

In the third week of January, during reading circle, Rose climbed onto my lap and sat there contentedly. Each day for the rest of the school year, Rose sat on my lap for those twenty minutes; doing so seemed to give her comfort. Rose was in my classroom through May.

She never spoke a word.

It has been forty years since I held Rose. She needed far more than I could give; had I known then what I have written in this chapter, I could have provided more support for her.

Other children have endured sexual abuse as Rose did or shootings as Pam and Reba did. Other children have been child soldiers, sex-trafficking victims, or survivors of natural disaster. Some traumas fit Lenore Terr's definition of type 1 trauma (a single, acute event) while others would be classified as type 2 (chronic and ongoing).[1] This chapter shares how nurturing children spiritually can foster resilience in them even in these most traumatic circumstances.

Common behaviors of children who have been removed from traumatic settings include oversensitivity, manipulation, aggression, bullying, disobedience, self-comforting, indiscriminate friendliness, lack of attachment, and overcompliance.[2] Common feelings these children share are grief, fear, confusion, shame, anxiety, anger, depression, sadness, and self-blame.[3] And common needs of children from these hard places are

---

[1]Lenore C. Terr, "Childhood Traumas: An Outline and Overview," *American Journal of Psychiatry* 148, no. 1 (1991): 10-20. Read more at traumadissociation.com/trauma-abuse.

[2]Thema Bryant-Davis, Monica U. Ellis, Elizabeth Burke-Maynard, Nathan Moon, Pamela A. Counts, and Gera Anderson, "Religiosity, Spirituality, and Trauma Recovery in the Lives of Children and Adolescents," *Professional Psychology: Research and Practice* 43, no. 4 (2012): 306-14; Emily Crawford, Margaret O'Dougherty Wright, and Ann S. Masten, "Resilience and Spirituality in Youth," in *The Handbook of Spiritual Development in Childhood and Adolescence*, ed. Eugene C. Roehlkepartain, Pamela E. King, Linda M. Wagener, and Peter L. Benson (Thousand Oaks, CA: Sage, 2006), 355-70; Nathan Chiroma, "Providing Mentoring for Orphans and Vulnerable Children in Internally Displaced Person Camps: The Case of Northern Nigeria," *HTS Teologiese Studies/Theological Studies* 72, no. 1 (October 2016): doi.org/10.4102/hts.v72i1.3544; James Garbarino and Claire Bedard, "Spiritual Challenges to Children Facing Violent Trauma," *Childhood* 3, no. 4 (1996): 467-78; Francis Grossman, Lynn Sorsoli, and Maryam Kia-Kealing, "A Gale Force Wind: Meaning Making by Male Survivors of Childhood Sexual Abuse," *American Journal of Orthopsychiatry* 76 (2006): 434-43; Ann Masten, *Ordinary Magic: Resilience in Development* (New York: Guilford Press, 2015); Krystal T. Simmons and Denika Y. Douglas, "After the Storm: Helping Children Cope with Trauma after Natural Disasters," *Communique* 46, no. 5 (January 1, 2018): 23-25.

[3]Bryant-Davis et al., "Religiosity, Spirituality, and Trauma Recovery"; Crawford, Wright, and

safety, hope, security, structure, boundaries, compassion, and respect.[4] In addition, they often need assistance in making meaning of their experiences, revisiting and possibly adjusting their understanding of God, and dealing with forgiveness issues.[5]

HOW SPIRITUALITY CAN BE A PROTECTIVE FACTOR

Resilience researchers in the 1980s began to link religion, faith, and spirituality to good outcomes in those who had experienced negative life circumstances.[6] More recent research is determining how and why religious or spiritual resources may cultivate resilience in those who have survived trauma.[7]

Crawford, Wright, and Masten's chapter on resilience and spirituality in the internationally recognized 2006 text *The Handbook of Spirituality Development in Childhood and Adolescence* offers a rich discussion of the ways religion or spirituality might operate in resilience. The authors group religious and spiritual channels into four categories:

- Attachment relationships
- Social support
- Guidelines for conduct and moral values
- Personal growth and development[8]

Under these four categories they describe twenty-seven different processes, some of which are explicitly religious, some specifically spiritual, some which are both. When a family loses a child, the family's religious community typically comes around that family offering much social

---

Masten, "Resilience and Spirituality"; Chiroma, "Providing Mentoring for Orphans"; Garbarino and Bedard, "Spiritual Challenges to Children"; Grossman, Sorsoli, and Kia-Kealing, "Male Survivors"; Masten, *Ordinary Magic*; Simmons and Douglas, "Helping Children Cope."

[4]Bryant-Davis et al., "Religiosity, Spirituality, and Trauma Recovery"; Crawford, Wright, and Masten, "Resilience and Spirituality"; Chiroma, "Providing Mentoring for Orphans"; Garbarino and Bedard, "Spiritual Challenges to Children"; Grossman, Sorsoli, and Kia-Kealing, "A Gale Force Wind"; Masten, *Ordinary Magic*; Simmons and Douglas, "Helping Children Cope."

[5]Grossman, Sorsoli, and Kia-Kealing, "Male Survivors," in addition to sources listed in the previous footnote.

[6]See, e.g., Werner and Smith, *Vulnerable but Invincible: A Study of Resilient Children* in 1982; Garmezy and Rutter, eds., *Stress, Coping, and Development in Children* in 1983.

[7]Crawford, Wright, and Masten, "Resilience and Spirituality in Youth."

[8]Crawford, Wright, and Masten, "Resilience and Spirituality in Youth," 358.

support (one of the four categories above), visiting, counseling, bringing food, and arranging death and burial rituals. Possessing a relationship with a benevolent, loving spiritual being (attachment relationships category) could be both religious and spiritual, as could practicing such virtues as forgiveness and hope (values category), and making meaning of loss and trauma (personal growth and development category). Let's consider each of these.

Possessing a relationship with a benevolent, loving spiritual being. Having a relationship with God can help children thrive in ordinary as well as challenging circumstances. Such a relationship can promote positive coping strategies and reduce stress in children.[9] When asked how he dealt with his father being in prison, one child said, "I pray. It helps me calm down."[10]

Believing in a caring and compassionate higher power can be a source of strength and confidence for children (and adults) as they encounter trauma and endure its aftershocks. Children who know a God who is present, who understands the enormity of what they have experienced, who offers them unconditional love, who is at work bringing about justice, and who is orchestrating healing and restoration[11] possess the most powerful resilience armor possible. Children who experience such a relationship tend to cope better in stressful situations.[12] A child's belief that this higher power can affect change in their circumstances and can support and sustain them affords a deep sense of well-being.[13]

Leaning into forgiveness. Children who have been trafficked as sex workers or child soldiers—among the most traumatic situations possible—face an arduous recovery, one feature of which is forgiveness.

---

[9]Mark D. Holder, Ben Coleman, and Judi M. Wallace, "Spirituality, Religiousness, and Happiness in Children Aged 8-12 Years," *Journal of Happiness Studies* 11 (2010): 131-50; Ande Nesmith and Ebony Ruhland, "Children of Incarcerated Parents: Challenges and Resiliency, in Their Own Words," *Children and Youth Services Review* 30, no. 10 (2008): 1127.

[10]Nesmith and Ruhland, "Children of Incarcerated Parents," 1127.

[11]Thema Bryant-Davis, *Thriving in the Wake of Trauma: A Multicultural Guide* (Westport, CT: Praeger, 2005), 154-55.

[12]Crawford, Wright, and Masten, "Resilience and Spirituality"; Bryant-Davis et al., "Religiosity, Spirituality, and Trauma Recovery."

[13]Crawford, Wright, and Masten, "Resilience and Spirituality."

As one former child soldier said, "Papa God, please forgive me. I did not want to do it. They made me do it."[14] These children have a desperate need to know that God forgives them before they are able to begin the process of forgiving themselves and the eventual process of forgiving those who have used and abused them.

Self-blame is common in children emerging from a variety of difficult circumstances,[15] for example, children who have been sexually abused, children whose sibling has died by suicide, or children who survived a population-wide trauma in which others were killed. These children can be assured that they are not to blame, of course, but it may take years for them to feel that they are not in some way responsible for these losses.

Children sometimes misunderstand what forgiveness entails. They may believe they are required to forgive the one who wounded them immediately. Or that they should forgive so the transgressor feels better. They might think that forgiveness means pretending that what the person did to them wasn't really that bad or that the offense could even be seen as helpful. [16]

In 1944, when Eva Kor and her ten-year-old twin sister arrived at Auschwitz, they were taken to a special facility where Dr. Josef Mengele and his team performed medical experiments on fifteen hundred sets of twins. Eva remembers that at one point she was injected with some unknown formula that made her very ill; she was placed in the infirmary, where her fever spiked and her body began to fail.[17] Though Eva and her sister survived Auschwitz, her parents and older siblings did not.

Over the next three decades, Eva strove to move past the deep grief, loss, and trauma she and her sister had endured. In her middle adult years, she began to realize that wholeness and hope would come if she could help others dealing with such grief and loss. Eventually she began

---

[14]Stephanie Goins, "The Place of Forgiveness in the Reintegration of Child Soldiers in Sierra Leone," in *Nurturing Children's Spirituality: Christian Perspectives and Best Practices*, ed. Holly C. Allen (Eugene, OR: Cascade, 2008), 297.

[15]Grossman et al., "A Gale Force Wind."

[16]Bryant-Davis et al., "Religiosity, Spirituality, and Trauma Recovery."

[17]Eva Kor and Lisa Buccieri, *Surviving the Angel of Death: The True Story of a Mengele Twin in Auschwitz* (Terra Haute, IN: Tanglewood, 2012).

the journey toward forgiveness that she knew to be necessary. She forgave the perpetrators of the crimes against her, meeting with Dr. Hans Münch, an Auschwitz physician who had known Dr. Mengele, and giving him a letter of forgiveness. Later Eva wrote, "I had the power to heal the pain imposed on me in Auschwitz by forgiving the people who imposed that pain."[18]

We can teach children who have been hurt by others about forgiveness. We can help them see that forgiveness is a process—not an immediate requirement for going forward—that a little progress is good, and that fuller forgiveness may come eventually.[19] And we can help the child see that forgiving the offender will help the child begin to heal. A key message Eva Kor offered when she spoke to survivors of trauma was this: "Forgive your worst enemy and forgive anybody who has hurt you—it will heal your soul and set you free."[20]

Making meaning of loss and trauma. One of the questions Miguel, who survived the Sandy Hook school shooting, asked was, "Why did this happen?"

Trauma represents an enormous challenge to anyone's understanding of the purpose and meaning of life but especially to children's. When children believe in a benevolent loving spiritual being who exists to protect them, experiencing trauma can cause cognitive—or perhaps we should say *spiritual*—dissonance.[21]

Adults have had more opportunity to construct a substantial framework of meaning, and they have had many more years to validate and affirm their core beliefs about life and purpose.[22] Furthermore, the reasoning skills adults possess to navigate the trauma-to-meaning challenge are less developed in children. Children simply have limited experience making meaning of the world at all. Consequently, they are more

---

[18]Eva Kor, "Eva Kor Statement at the Trial of Oscar Groening," CANDLES Holocaust Museum and Education Center, April 22, 2015, candlesholocaustmuseum.org/learn/oskar-groening.html.

[19]Bryant-Davis et al., "Religiosity, Spirituality, and Trauma Recovery."

[20]Kor and Buccieri, *Surviving the Angel of Death*, 134.

[21]Garbarino and Bedard, "Spiritual Challenges to Children," 470-71.

[22]Garbarino and Bedard, "Spiritual Challenges to Children," 471.

likely to develop posttraumatic stress disorder[23] after a traumatic event than adults.[24]

Well-known child psychiatrist and author Robert Coles notes that children have a deep need to understand what has happened to them and why it happened. He says that to navigate this path to understanding, children tap into the spiritual values they have absorbed and the religious lives they have experienced.[25] Several studies have offered support for the idea that religion and spirituality can provide children and adolescents a sense of meaning and purpose in life—both part of Ann Masten's protective factor of faith, hope, and the belief that life has meaning.[26]

FOSTERING SPIRITUALITY IN CHILDREN WHO HAVE EXPERIENCED TRAUMA

Most children recovering from life-altering, traumatic experiences need one-on-one trauma counseling or trauma-focused cognitive behavioral therapy, which may (or may not) lean into the spiritual factors that can foster healing.[27]

---

[23]Posttraumatic stress disorder (PTSD) is a "specific type of anxiety disorder that can occur after a horrifying traumatic event": Sherry Grogan and Kathleen Murphy, "Anticipatory Stress Response in PTSD: Extreme Stress in Children," *Journal of Child and Adolescent Psychiatric Nursing* 24 (2011): 58. Common characteristics of PTSD can be replaying or re-experiencing the trauma through vivid memories, nightmares or flashbacks, avoiding anything related to the trauma, emotional numbing, and hyperarousal, such as irritability, constant fear, or continual scanning for threats; Holly R. Wethington et al., "The Effectiveness of Interventions to Reduce Psychological Harm from Traumatic Events Among Children and Adolescents: A Systematic Review," *American Journal of Preventive Medicine* 35, no. 3 (2008): 287-313.

[24]Jonathan Davidson and Rebecca Smith, "Traumatic Experiences in Psychiatric Outpatients," *Journal of Traumatic Stress Studies* 3 (1990): 459-75.

[25]Robert Coles, *The Spiritual Life of Children* (Boston: Houghton Mifflin, 1990).

[26]For a full discussion of Ann Masten's work on resilience, see chapter two.

[27]Because of the alienation that has historically existed between the behavioral sciences and religion, the spiritual concerns of clients have often been neglected in the counseling world. Counseling education programs have encouraged future counselors to practice self-reflection and increase their self-awareness in order to reduce bias when working with clients, but counselors are sometimes unwilling or feel unqualified to discuss spiritual issues with clients. See, e.g., P. Scot Richards and Akken E. Bergin, *A Spiritual Strategy for Counseling and Psychotherapy*, 2nd ed. (Washington, DC: American Psychological Association, 2005); Michael J. Vogel, Mark R. McMinn, Mary A. Peterson, and Kathleen Gathercoal, "Examining Religion and Spirituality as Diversity Training: A Multidimensional Look at Training in the American Psychological Association," *Professional Psychology: Research and Practice* 44, no, 3 (2013): 158-67; Scott S. Young, Marsha Wiggins-Frame, and Craig S. Cashwell, "Spirituality and Counselor Competence: A National Survey of American Counseling Association Members," *Journal of Counseling &*

Beyond personal counseling, children will need strong parental support as they rebuild their lives (see chapter four). Parents are often the most crucial influences in this rebuilding process, though if the parents themselves were also impacted by the trauma, their ability to provide the support their children need may be compromised. Other support may be available, for example, some children may live in readjustment or rehabilitation centers or participate in recovery groups following the trauma. Even being part of a church or afterschool program can help children.[28] The practices shared below can be used by parents, grandparents, teachers, and social workers as well as psychologists and counselors in religious or nonreligious settings. These activities were designed to create opportunities for children to tap into some of Crawford, Wright, and Masten's twenty-seven processes that nurture spirituality and can promote resilience. Some of the activities, for example, foster children's connection with God (as the child understands God); some encourage discussion concerning forgiveness or hope; others provide openings for making meaning of their traumatic experiences.

These practices were gleaned from the many sources already cited in this chapter and were utilized over the past few years with children whose parents were incarcerated, children living in generational poverty, children who had fled nations in civil war, and children struggling with racial inequities.[29]

Reading children's books. Children who survive traumatic experiences sometimes experience such spiritual challenges as feeling unworthy of God's intervention or feeling tested by God. They may wonder how God could allow such abuse or loss to happen, or they may blame

---

Development 85, no. 1 (2007): 47-52; Christine A. Courtois, "Spiritual Challenges Resulting from Trauma: Implications for Inclusive Psychotherapy," in *APA Handbook of Trauma Psychology: Foundations in Knowledge,* ed. Steven N. Gold (Washington, DC: American Psychological Association, 2017), 559-72.

[28]As the previous footnote indicates, since many counselors are unwilling or feel unqualified to discuss spiritual issues with clients, sometimes ordinary caregivers will be the only people children may have who are willing to enter the spiritual realm.

[29]For the past five years, students participating in a children's spirituality course at Lipscomb University have mentored children whose parents were incarcerated, children in an afterschool program in a lower socioeconomic neighborhood, children in an afterschool program for refugee families, and children in an afterschool program at a Christian academy.

God for their suffering.[30] Providing safe places for children to raise questions about God, express their fears, doubts, and even anger, or simply talk about their experiences is part of the process of spiritually engaging the trauma. Reading children's books creates opportunities for such discussions to arise.

Olivia, a Lipscomb student who mentored in an afterschool program for refugees, describes an important breakthrough with twelve-year-old Nahla from Democratic Republic of Congo that occurred while they were reading a book together.[31] The book was titled *Nana Upstairs and Nana Downstairs*, about a little boy named Tommy who loves and eventually loses his great-grandmother, then his grandmother.[32] When Olivia asked Nahla how she connected to the book, Nahla responded that when her family had been fleeing their country when she was six, her twin sister had been struck by a car and killed as her whole family watched. Nahla also told Olivia that she didn't think God heard her prayers because, when her sister lay dying by the side of the road, Nahla had begged God not to let her die. Olivia listened compassionately while Nahla shared about her sister's death as well as the resulting spiritual dissonance she had been feeling since she lost her. For many weeks, Olivia had been empathizing and listening to Nahla, and thus, when they read this tender children's book, Nahla saw Olivia as a safe person whom she could trust, someone with whom she could share her doubts about prayer and God.[33]

When reading this same book, Ella, whose mom was in prison, told her mentor she didn't have any grandparents but was like the little boy in the story because her daddy had died the previous year. As she shared this, her mentor began to see why Ella saw herself as a "good shepherd" for her younger sisters. Another child whose mom was in prison identified with the *Nana Upstairs* book in another way: she told her mentor

---

[30]Bryant-Davis et al., "Religiosity, Spirituality, and Trauma Recovery," 310.

[31]The children's names in this chapter are pseudonyms.

[32]Tomie dePaola, *Nana Upstairs and Nana Downstairs* (New York: Puffin Press, 2000).

[33]Nahla's story was first told in Holly Catterton Allen, "Resilience, Trauma, and Children's Spirituality" (with Lipscomb students Kaylee Frank and Megan Larry), in *Bridging Theory and Practice in Children's Spirituality*, ed. Mimi Larson and Robert Keeley (Grand Rapids, MI: Zondervan, 2020), 136. Used by permission of Zondervan, www.zondervan.com.

that her grandmother had diabetes and that she helped her grandmother reach things she could not access.[34]

Creating a narrative. Trauma counselors sometimes recommend that children write, draw, or tell their stories as they cope with traumatic experiences in their lives.[35] These stories can show events leading up to the situation, the trauma event itself, the rescue, or the resolution. Drawing their stories can serve as vehicles for children to ask questions about God, hope, death, or guilt. Creating a visual or written narrative can help children navigate the crucial process of meaning making that is so fundamentally interconnected with resilience.[36]

The Lipscomb University students who participated in the afterschool refugee program were asked to refrain from asking probing questions about the children's refugee experiences, but if the children themselves initiated the conversation, the college students were encouraged to participate in the conversations. The following story illustrates how these refugee children are making meaning of the experiences they have suffered and the losses they have sustained.

On our last day of mentoring the refugee children, each child (as well as their mentor) drew their family tree. Nahla drew her family standing under a tree: her parents, herself, her older brother and sister who had escaped with the family, and her two younger siblings who'd been born since the family arrived in the United States. She also drew her sister who had died, Ninah; she placed her in the upper corner of the picture with wings and a smile on her face. Nahla told her mentor, "We don't ever talk about Ninah at home, but I know she is here; she sees me and knows I am here and that I miss her and I haven't forgotten her." This particular

---

[34]Holly Catterton Allen (with Lipscomb students Carly Brandvold, Alana Lauck, and Erin Trageser), "Nurturing Spiritual Development in Children Whose Parents Are Incarcerated," in *Formation and Culture: From Theory to Practice in Ministry with Children,* ed. Benjamin Espinoza, James Estep, and Shirley Morgenthaler (Eugene, OR: Wipf & Stock/Pickwick, 2018).

[35]Donald F. Walker, Jennifer B. Reese, John P. Hughes, and Melissa J. Troskie, "Addressing Religious and Spiritual Issues in Trauma-Focused Cognitive Behavior Therapy for Children and Adolescents," *Professional Psychology: Research and Practice* 41 (2010): 178.

[36]Masten, *Ordinary Magic.* Of course, *pressing* a child to draw or tell their story would never be appropriate; providing oblique opportunities as illustrated in this chapter and throughout this book allows children to lean into their experiences if and when they are ready to do so.

story poignantly illustrates the child-self, child-others, and child-God relationships that contribute to resilience.

Eight Days: A Story of Haiti tells the story of a young boy who is trapped under his house for eight long days after Haiti's 2010 earthquake.[37] To keep up his courage, he daydreams about flying kites, shooting marbles, and playing hide-and-seek until he is rescued. It is an inspiring, hope-filled story of a child surviving a tragedy with resilience.

Numerous accounts written by adults of their childhood trauma are available, for example, Ishmael Beah's account of his years as a child soldier[38] and Thida Butt Mam's biography of her childhood in Cambodia under the Khmer Rouge.[39] For many children, telling their stories of loss and grief offers one way for them to gain a sense of meaning in their lives.

Victor Frankl believed that making meaning, particularly amid suffering, is necessary for resilience, and part of making meaning for Frankl was telling of his experiences at Auschwitz in his classic work *Man's Search for Meaning*.[40] More recently, others have also linked the ability to tell a coherent and meaningful account of one's life to resilience in the face of adversity.[41] They go so far as to say that this ability in children and youth is the most important foundation for resilience.[42]

Processing the trauma with other children who experienced it. *Story of a Storm: A Book About Hurricane Katrina*[43] is a fascinating children's book written and illustrated by thirty five-to-thirteen-year-olds and their teacher Reola Visser, who lived in Long Beach on the Mississippi Gulf Coast and survived the hurricane. The children's collage art and pithy

[37]Edwidge Danticat, *Eight Days: A Story of Haiti* (New York: Orchard Books, 2010).

[38]Ishmael Beah, *A Long Way Home: Memoirs of a Boy Soldier* (New York: Sarah Crichton Books, 2007).

[39]Thida Butt Mam, *To Destroy You Is No Loss* (Auke Bay, AK: East/West Bridge Publishing House, 1998).

[40]Victor Frankl, *Man's Search for Meaning* (Boston: Beacon Press, 1959).

[41]B. J. Cohler, "The Life Story and the Study of Resilience and Response to Adversity," *Journal of Narrative and Life History* 1, nos. 2-3 (1991): 169-200; Garbarino and Bedard, "Children Facing Violent Trauma."

[42]Garbarino and Bedard, "Children Facing Violent Trauma."

[43]Reona Visser, *Story of a Storm: A Book About Hurricane Katrina* (Brandon, MS: Quail Ridge Press, 2006).

sentences depict their experiences before ("We tried to make our house safe"), during ("Katrina's winds were terrible, and blew things to pieces"), and after the hurricane—living in FEMA housing ("Our new home was not the same, but it was a home").

Writing and illustrating this book together helped this teacher and these children process their experiences, their losses, their adjustments, their survival—all of which are spiritual processes connected to resilience.

Abby Mosby is the director of Nations Ministry, the afterschool program for the refugee children who paired up with Lipscomb students in mentorship relationships. Mosby says one of the great advantages of an afterschool program designed for refugee children is that the children can connect with others who have been through traumas similar to theirs. Because these children are learning a new language and adapting to a new culture, they often struggle academically and socially; when they exhibit emotional fragility or even public meltdowns, there is less judgment in this setting since the other children are managing comparable struggles. "This can be healing for refugee children and can help them establish a strong sense of belonging that they may have difficulty finding elsewhere in their country of refuge," Mosby says.[44]

Spiritual practices in Christian settings. In settings where the care children receive is explicitly Christian, caregivers can utilize more overtly religious processes. One review of thirty-four studies of childhood abuse and spirituality suggests that personal religious and spiritual faith can moderate the degree to which some participants experience PTSD and other troubling symptoms associated with childhood trauma.[45] For example, in one study of childhood abuse, the participants' religious beliefs and practices such as prayer became part of the healing process.[46] When questions about God arise ("Why did God let this happen?" or "Why

---

[44]Lipscomb student Kaylee Frank interviewed Abby Mosby and included this material in her senior capstone paper in February 2018. Used with permission.

[45]Donald F. Walker, Henri Webb Reid, Tiffany O'Neill, and Lindsay Brown, "Changes in Personal Religion/Spirituality during and after Childhood Abuse: A Review and Synthesis," *Psychological Trauma: Theory, Research, Practice, and Policy* 1 (2009): 130-45.

[46]Walker, Reid, O'Neill, and Brown, "Changes in Personal Religion/Spirituality during and after Childhood Abuse."

didn't God stop it?"), one good response is to ask children if they would like to write or dictate a letter to God, perhaps adding an illustration. This process once again creates an opportunity for the child to revisit the child-God relationship and engage the meaning-making process.

A source of trauma not addressed previously in this book is that African American children in the United States begin to pick up on bias and racism in early elementary years. Nichelle, an African American eight-year-old, attended the afterschool program at a predominantly white private Christian school that was a recent setting for the mentoring portion of the children's spirituality course I teach.

Nichelle bounced into our mentoring setting the first two weeks full of excitement, describing her relationship with God in colorful, winning language. According to her mentor, Kaya—also African American—the third week was different. Nichelle walked in slowly, exuding sadness, clearly deep in thought. Nichelle explained to Kaya that she thought her friends were treating her differently because she is African American. In her end-of-semester reflection on her mentoring experience, Kaya said Nichelle "thought she was not good enough for her friends because they had begun to notice the evident physical differences between her and them. More than once Nichelle said, 'I love being African American, but . . . '"

In each of the afterschool settings in which the Lipscomb students have mentored, they ask several prepared questions of their mentees over the course of the semester. Some of the questions include: "Can you tell me about a time when you felt surprised or amazed about God? Sorry or guilty toward God? Happy about God? Sad about God? Scared about God? Angry at God? Ever feel love for God?"[47]

When Kaya asked Nichelle, "Have you ever felt angry toward God?" Nichelle responded, "Yes, I feel angry at God because he made me African American; being African American is nice but other people disrespect us and make us feel like we aren't good enough."[48]

---

[47]These specific questions about the child's feelings about God derive primarily from David Heller's classic research, which he chronicles in his book *The Children's God* (Chicago: University of Chicago Press, 1988).

[48]Story used with written permission from Kaya Coleman.

As these stories illustrate, Nichelle, Nahla, Ella, Tyrone, and the other children in the afterschool programs where Lipscomb students have mentored were given many opportunities to speak truth about their relationships with God, others, and themselves. These conversations offered safes space to ask questions, engage with empathetic listeners, think about God, and process their feelings—which contribute to healing, understanding, and hope.

Though it has been forty years, I have not forgotten Pam, Reba, and Rose and the circumstances surrounding the trauma they survived. Undoubtedly, they have not forgotten their trauma either. If I were to encounter another Pam, Reba, or Rose in my life, I would now know some ways to help them make meaning, forgive, and lean into God (as they understand God).

For those who work or volunteer in a situation where many children are present (such as a classroom, children's ministry, daycare center, or afterschool program), it is likely that a few children will exhibit some of the characteristics listed earlier in this chapter that may signal their experience of trauma: oversensitivity, manipulation, aggression, bullying, disobedience, self-comforting, indiscriminate friendliness, lack of grief (emotional numbness), fear, confusion, shame, anxiety, anger, depression, sadness, or self-blame.[49]

Since most teachers, afterschool workers, volunteers, and children's ministers are not licensed counselors, they will not be the primary support for these children; however, the ideas below offer ways to provide an environment for healing:

- Create a safe environment; establish a sense of safety; be calm and relaxed.
- Give extra reassurance and care.
- Monitor your own responses and (exhibited) emotions; adult behavior and attitudes strongly influence children's ability to recover.

---

[49]Bryant-Davis et al., "Religiosity, Spirituality, and Trauma Recovery"; Crawford, Wright, and Masten, "Resilience and Spirituality"; Chiroma, "Providing Mentoring for Orphans"; Garbarino and Bedard, "Spiritual Challenges to Children"; Grossman et al., "A Gale Force Wind"; Masten, *Ordinary Magic*; Simmons and Douglas, "After the Storm."

- Ask about feelings; let them know that feeling upset is okay and is normal and acceptable.
- Monitor media exposure.
- Consider the ideas in this chapter (and other ideas in the book)— reading children's books, writing a letter to God, drawing a family tree, walking a labyrinth, asking wondering questions, offering quiet space, and so on.
- If after a few months a child continues to have emotional or behavioral problems after the trauma, you may wish to consider recommending professional help for the child.

CONNECTING TRAUMA, CHILDREN'S SPIRITUALITY, AND RESILIENCE

Bryant-Davis and her coauthors open their article on spirituality and trauma recovery saying that spiritual coping mechanisms such as meaning making and possessing a sense of hope and a sense of belonging contribute to "decreased depressive symptoms, greater self-esteem, and overall greater life satisfaction,"[50] all of which reflect resilience.

One final story about Kaya and Nichelle. Over the remaining weeks of their time together, Kaya and Nichelle continued their sensitive, crucial discussions. Kaya's personal history and keen interpersonal awareness played an invaluable role in the grappling process Nichelle was struggling through. Nichelle was dealing at a deep spiritual level with the child-self relationship (unworthiness), the child-others relationship (friends), and the child-God relationship ("I feel angry at God because . . ."). Near the end of their time together (the eighth week), the planned activity was to ask the children to draw God in any way they wished.

Nichelle drew a Black Jesus and a White Jesus. Below the Black Jesus, Nichelle wrote, "Black Jesus protects Black people"; underneath White Jesus, Nichelle wrote, "White Jesus protects White people." Nichelle's

---

[50]Bryant-Davis et al., "Religiosity, Spirituality, and Trauma Recovery," 306, citing Marie Good and Teena Willoughby, "Adolescence as a Sensitive Period for Spiritual Development," *Child Development Perspectives* 2 (2008): 32-37; Holder et al., "Spirituality, Religiousness, and Happiness."

time with Kaya offered multiple opportunities for her to wrestle with the realities of her life in a way that connected directly to her spirituality—that is, the child-self relationship, child-others relationship, and, very importantly, the child-God relationship. And it also created openings for Nichelle to begin that complex lifelong process of making meaning.

Intentional spiritual practices with children can help them bring their religious beliefs, their relationship with God, and their understanding of how the world works to the daunting task of processing their experiences of trauma and loss. Restoration and healing will likely be a lifelong undertaking for these children, even for children who receive the support they need from counselors, ministers, parents, and their community. Trauma is simply hard; just as it takes a long time to fully recover from physical wounds sustained in a devastating automobile accident—even with the best care, so it is with trauma. Nevertheless, it has been well-documented that protective factors including spiritual practices can have a moderating effect on children's outcomes after exposure to adverse experiences, even trauma.[51]

Introducing children to elemental spiritual tools can contribute to the resilience they need to heal, survive, and thrive, and ultimately can equip them to continue to draw on their budding spirituality as they live into the rest of their lives with resilience.

---

[51]Goldstein and Brooks, *Handbook of Resilience in Children*; Masten, *Ordinary Magic*; Tracie O. Afifi and Harriet L. Macmillan, "Resilience Following Child Maltreatment: A Review of Protective Factors," *Canadian Journal of Psychiatry* 56, no. 5 (2011): 266-72.

CHAPTER ELEVEN

Grief and Loss

ALLIE AND HER TWIN BROTHER, Aaron, are twelve years old. Their dad moved out of the house about a year ago and now lives in a condo on the other side of town. Their parents' divorce was final about six months ago. Their mom is sad and still cries in her room almost every evening. Their dad says that things just didn't work out; he also says he will make sure they have what they need. Allie and Aaron visit their dad every other weekend. Allie wonders if maybe her mom and dad will get back together. Aaron is trying to step up and be the "man of the house," taking on some of his dad's chores like taking the garbage to the curb on Thursdays. They still go to the same church they always have, but mostly no one mentions their dad or the divorce. Their mom recently moved to full-time work from her previous part-time position. Allie and Aaron are beginning to realize things will never be the same.

When Molly was ten, she was diagnosed with leukemia. For the next three years, her life and her family's life centered on her medical care and her recovery. She was hospitalized for a few weeks, then received most of her care as an outpatient, which allowed her to attend school most of the time. Initially Molly lost her hair, and later, some of the medications caused her to gain weight. These medical situations yielded some name-calling and bullying from schoolmates. Molly asked her mom why God would allow this to happen to her.

Ella is the oldest of three children. Ella's dad died a year ago from a drug overdose and her mother is in prison; she and her sisters are living with family friends. She told her mentor, "I am afraid of dying; I have to be here to take care of my sisters."

The previous chapter considered various severe traumas children sometimes face. This chapter will summarize how to spiritually support children who have endured the grief and loss that accompanies parental divorce, chronic or terminal illness, or the death of a sibling or parent. Children of divorce often feel overlooked, confused, guilty, and fearful; children who are seriously or terminally ill may feel helpless, lonely, and fearful; and children who have lost a parent or sibling to death often feel angry, sad, and fearful. Those in the helping professions who work with these children have been unsure how to incorporate spiritual approaches in the healing process.[1]

This chapter offers specific ways to help these children in their relationships with self, others, and God (as they understand God). Our desire for children whose parents divorce, children who are chronically ill, and children who lose a parent or sibling to death is that they will move into their adult years with resilience—that is, that though these significant losses will continue to inform their lives, they will not define them or compromise their ability to move into successful, fruitful lives with hope.

CHILDREN OF DIVORCE

Each year since 1973, a million children become involved in divorce. Judith Wallerstein, Elizabeth Marquardt, and Mavis Hetherington have conducted extensive studies of the effects of divorce on children and the young adults they become. Though 20 to 25 percent of children of divorce experience serious social and emotional problems,[2] these authors maintain that the other 75 to 80 percent are deeply affected as well. Most children of divorce, even those who go on to lead outwardly successful

---

[1]P. Scot Richards and Akken E. Bergin, *A Spiritual Strategy for Counseling and Psychotherapy*, 2nd ed. (Washington, DC: American Psychological Association, 2005); Michael J. Vogel, Mark R. McMinn, Mary A. Peterson, and Kathleen Gathercoal, "Examining Religion and Spirituality as Diversity Training: A Multidimensional Look at Training in the American Psychological Association," *Professional Psychology: Research and Practice* 44, no, 3 (2013): 158-67; Scott S. Young, Marsha Wiggins-Frame, and Craig S. Cashwell, "Spirituality and Counselor Competence: A National Survey of American Counseling Association Members," *Journal of Counseling & Development* 85, no. 1 (2007): 47-52.

[2]Mavis E. Hetherington and John Kelly, *For Better or Worse: Divorce Reconsidered* (New York: W. W. Norton, 2002), 9.

lives, typically experience confusion, isolation, and suffering; they are often deeply absorbed in their parents' needs and vulnerabilities; and they tend to confront complex moral questions earlier than their peers.[3] They are often alone and lonely. They may keep secrets for their parents, become protective of their parents, and feel emotionally and physically less safe than peers from intact families.[4] They feel less protected, less cared for, and less comforted.[5] They feel frightened about the present and the future; they feel overlooked, guilty, and fearful.[6]

Though psychologists might identify these outcomes as interpersonal or psychological in nature (and they are), they are also spiritual. When we consider our definition of children's spirituality—their relationship with self, others, and God—the connections are evident.

Marquardt in particular, due to the nature of her study, which focused specifically on the moral and spiritual lives of children of divorce, frames some of her findings in spiritual terms, by which she means primarily the children's moral and religious lives as well as their understanding of God. Marquardt eloquently describes the winding, lonely, and sometimes surprising spiritual journeys of the children of divorce in her study (Marquardt herself was a child of divorce and uses the personal pronoun *we* as she identifies with her participants):

> Growing up we deal early and alone with profound losses and confront big questions of meaning. We search for explanations in a culture that too often denies our loss, dismissing our questions as cute or precocious or ignoring us altogether. We are child-sized old souls. When we come of age and leave home, we are less likely overall to be religious. We long for spirituality as much as our peers from intact families do, but loss, suffering, lack of trust in, and anger at our parents, and even anger at God are more defining qualities of our spiritual journey.[7]

---

[3]Elizabeth Marquardt, *Between Two Worlds: The Inner Lives of Children of Divorce* (New York: Three Rivers Press, 2005).
[4]Marquardt, *Between Two Worlds*, 32.
[5]Judith Wallerstein and Sandra Blakeslee, *Second Chances: Men, Women, and Children a Decade After Divorce* (Boston: Tickner & Fields, 1989), 23.
[6]Marquardt, *Between Two Worlds*; Judith S. Wallerstein and Sandra Blakeslee, *What About the Kids? Raising Your Children Before, During, and After Divorce* (New York: Hyperion, 2003).
[7]Marquardt, *Between Two Worlds*, 139.

HOW CAN WE SUPPORT CHILDREN OF DIVORCE IN THEIR SPIRITUAL JOURNEY?

Fewer than 10 percent of the participants in Wallerstein's studies reported that any adult spoke to them sympathetically as the divorce unfolded.[8] In fact, one of the more common observations in the literature addressing children and divorce is that children have no place to safely share their fears, concerns, burdens, anger, and frustrations, especially since some of those feelings are integrally related to one or both parents. Probably the most important thing one can do when spending time with children whose parents are divorcing or have divorced in the past few months (or years) is listen to their stories, allow their anger without reacting negatively, and acknowledge their experiences as their reality—without simply assuring them everything will be okay. What might this look like?

Writing a letter to God. Twelve-year-old Allie from the story earlier in this chapter wrote the following letter to God:

> Why did you let this happen? What am I supposed to do now? I can't make everything okay. I can't make my dad come back. I can't make my mom okay. She is sad all the time. What am I going to do? Why don't you make them love each other again?

This missive is hard to read; however, we know that children need to express their feelings to adults of their acquaintance and to God. They may not have safe places to share these thoughts. The simple exercise of writing a letter to God offers a safe place. Occasionally the children we have worked with in our afterschool mentoring sessions did not wish to show their letter to their mentor; even so, they have had the opportunity to talk with God. That opportunity can serve them well, contributing to the child-self and child-God relationship.

Drawing their family. One of the simplest ways for children to begin to share their stories is to have an opportunity to draw their family. In the fifteen years I have been teaching the children's spirituality course,

---

[8]Wallerstein and Blakeslee, *Second Chances*, 13.

my university students have mentored about two hundred children. This activity—drawing the child's family—has often yielded poignant conversations, particularly with children whose parents are divorced. One way we have found to help children consider whom to include in their picture is to offer this guideline: "Just draw who lives in your house or apartment." This helps children realize pets are allowed in their picture; sometimes it prompts the revelation of a detail that may not have surfaced yet—that Dad or Mom doesn't live in their house or that they live in two places: some weeks with Dad, some weeks with Mom.

As children draw those who live in their home, some draw a line down the middle of the paper, with Dad or Mom on the other side of the line; sometimes they draw two pictures showing who lives in their dad's house and who lives in their mom's house.

The mentors typically draw their own households as well, and when the children talk about their families, the mentors share their own drawings. Tender discussions have arisen when the university mentor shares that his or her parents are also divorced. The children sometimes ask questions about their mentor's situation. Whether further discussion ensues or not, one message is very clear: the child sees that their mentor has survived the family's divorce, is functioning, is attending college, and is managing life. That is a powerful—and much-needed—message.

Sometimes when the children share their family picture, they exhibit anger at their parents or at God; sometimes they confess fears. This setting can provide a safe place for children to talk about deep emotions, as they may not wish to share them with their mom or dad. Sharing their family's picture with a good listener can nurture the child-self, child-others, and child-God relationships that contribute to resilience.

CHILDREN FACING ILLNESS AND DEATH

In the United States, more than 13,000 children are diagnosed with cancer each year, another 13,000 children are diagnosed with type 1 diabetes annually, and 200,000 children live with either type 1 or type 2 diabetes. Nine million children suffer from asthma, and estimates of pediatric recurrent abdominal pain range from 0.3 percent to 18 percent of the population (225,000 to 13.5 million children).[9]

Children who face life-threatening illnesses can experience feelings of helplessness, inferiority, and inadequacy; they may lose a sense of normalcy and perhaps physical vigor. They must cope with changes in their relationships with parents, siblings, and friends and must reconsider future goals.[10] Each of these emotional, physical, and psychosocial consequences can lead to spiritual distress:

> Within the domain of the physical body, the experience of pain can lead individuals to intense spiritual inquiry regarding the meaning of suffering. Similarly, hopes, fears, problematic relationships with family members or schoolmates . . . or one's understanding of an illness and its medical care [are interconnected] with spirituality.[11]

The spiritual distress children experience may be accompanied by a sense of diminished hope and self-worth, which can negatively affect the healing process.[12]

There may not be opportunities for children to discuss their fears and concerns in a hospital setting due to a variety of constraints: inadequate pastoral staffing, insufficient training of healthcare professionals to recognize children's spiritual needs, and the fact that nurses and doctors must attend first and foremost to the acute physical needs of their patients. And, of course, children rarely announce spiritual needs; they can often say where something hurts, but they may not articulate well their fears about life and death, their loneliness, their sadness over their losses, or their wonderings about where God is in their time of need.[13] Consequently, children may be left alone to deal with their fears and confusion.

---

[9]Bruce E. Compas, Sarah S. Jaser, Madeleine J. Dunn, and Erin M. Rodrigues, "Coping with Chronic Illness in Childhood and Adolescence," *Annual Review of Clinical Psychology* 8 (2012): 455-80.

[10]Dynnette Hart and Dawn Schneider, "Spiritual Care for Children with Cancer," *Seminars in Oncology Nursing* 13, no. 4 (1997): 263-70.

[11]Chris Feudtner, Jeff Haney, and Martha A. Dimmers, "Spiritual Care Needs of Hospitalized Children and Their Families: A National Survey of Pastoral Care Providers' Perceptions," *Pediatrics* 111, no.1 (January 2003): e68.

[12]Hart and Schneider, "Spiritual Care for Children with Cancer."

[13]Emily Hufton, "Parting Gifts: The Spiritual Needs of Children," *Journal of Child Health Care* 10, no. 3 (2006): 240-50.

Pediatric nurses Dynnette Hart and Dawn Schneider write that spiritual care includes activities that help children find meaning and purpose and transcend beyond the self.[14] When Jerome Berryman worked with chronically and terminally ill children at Texas Children's Hospital in the 1980s, he began to recognize that children grapple with the same deep issues that adults confront: the awareness of death, the need for meaning, the threat to their freedom, and being alone.[15] As Berryman notes, "It is hard to pretend that children are not aware of their existential limits in a pediatric hospital."[16] In fact, Berryman says that the first people who really saw what Godly Play could do for children were the child life workers at Texas Children's Hospital.[17]

Medical professionals give children language to discuss questions about their physical illness by offering them a doctor's kit facsimile or taking them to visit the operating room before their surgery. Just so, child life specialists, parents, and hospital chaplains can help give children language to discuss their troubling questions by sharing a Godly Play story. Some of Berryman's scripts are especially suited to non-faith-based children's hospitals (or public schools and other secular settings). For example, the introduction to the Good Shepherd parable says, "There was once someone who said such amazing things and did such wonderful things that people followed him. They couldn't help it. They wanted to know who he was, so they just had to ask him. Once when they asked him who he was, he said, 'I am the Good Shepherd.'"[18] There is no mention of the name of Jesus in this story's script.[19] The wondering questions that follow this parable include: "I wonder if the sheep are happy inside this place? I wonder where this place could

---

[14]Hart and Schneider, "Spiritual Care for Children with Cancer," 263.

[15]Jerome W. Berryman, "The Chaplain's Strange Language: A Unique Contribution to the Health Care Team," in *Life, Faith, Hope, and Magic: The Chaplaincy in Pediatric Cancer Care,* ed. Jan van Eys and Edward J. Mahnke (Austin: University of Texas Press, 1985); Jerome W. Berryman, *Teaching Godly Play: How to Mentor the Spiritual Development of Children,* 2nd ed. (Denver: Morehouse Education Resources, 2009), 46.

[16]Jerome W. Berryman, *The Spiritual Guidance of Children: Montessori, Godly Play, and the Future* (New York: Morehouse Publishing, 2013), 77.

[17]Berryman, *Spiritual Guidance of Children*; for a fuller explanation of Godly Play, see chapter nine.

[18]Jerome W. Berryman, *The Complete Guide to Godly Play: Twenty Presentations for Winter,* vol. 3 (Jerome Berryman, 2002), 82.

[19]When I share this story in Christian settings, I identify the "someone who said amazing things" and the Good Shepherd as Jesus.

really be? I wonder if you have ever come close to such a place? I wonder if you ever had to go through a place of danger? I wonder how you got through?"[20] After these open-ended questions, the children are given time to work (play) with the sheep, the sheepfold, the Good Shepherd, the wolf, the ordinary shepherd, and "places of danger" and to ask their own wondering questions. This individual play time offers indirect opportunities for children contending with chronic or terminal illness to address their fears and concerns.

Godly Play teaches children the art of story and wonder to help them become more fully aware of the mystery of God's presence in their lives, thus nurturing their relationship with God (as they understand God). Wondering can tap into personal concerns regarding aloneness, meaning, and death, along the way contributing to that elusive quality—resilience. Besides sharing Godly Play stories, reading children's books, drawing families and feelings, and simply listening, providing spiritual care can include activities such as holding, comforting, and encouraging parental participation in the child's care; all of these activities will assist in nurturing the child's and family's spiritual life.[21]

CHILDREN COPING WITH LOSS OF A PARENT OR SIBLING

The death of a parent or a sibling is one of the most painful events that can occur in a child's life. Approximately 1.5 million children are living in a single-parent household because of the death of one parent.[22] In one study that examined grieving in schools, classroom teachers reported that students who had lost a parent or guardian typically exhibited difficulty concentrating in class, withdrawal or disengagement, less class participation, absenteeism, decrease in quality of work, and less reliability in turning in assignments.[23]

---

[20]Berryman, *Complete Guide to Godly Play*, 85.

[21]Hart and Schneider, "Spiritual Care for Children with Cancer."

[22]Darrell A. Owens, "Recognizing the Needs of Bereaved Children in Palliative Care," *Journal of Hospice & Palliative Nursing* 10, no. 1 (2008): 14.

[23]"Grieving in Schools: Nationwide Survey Among Classroom Teachers on Childhood Bereavement" (survey conducted by New York Life Foundation and American Federation of Teachers,

The death of a sibling is somewhat different from the loss of a parent, but the deep grief that accompanies such a loss is just as profound. It is estimated that 73,000 children die every year in the United States, and of those children, 83 percent have surviving siblings.[24] Losing a sibling entails the loss of a role model, a friend, a confidante, and a playmate.[25] Siblings of children dying of cancer often feel left out, rejected, or isolated.[26] Children may feel guilty for surviving the death of a sibling. They may also feel guilty if they are having fun or not feeling very sad after a family member has died.[27]

The school grieving study cited earlier found that, at the time of the study, seven in ten teachers had at least one student in their class(es) who had lost a parent, guardian, sibling, or close friend in the past year.[28] Teachers, children's ministers, child caregivers, and others who work with children will eventually come in contact with a child who has lost a parent or sibling to death. Yet Western cultures have tended toward a "death-denying and grief-avoiding" outlook, especially in regard to children, signaling that they should be protected "from the harshness of loss and death."[29] According to Alan Wolfelt, well-known death educator and grief counselor, children are frequently referred to as the "forgotten mourners," partly due to this death-denying cultural norm but also because adults may be grieving their own loss and be uncertain how to support their grieving child.[30]

2012), www.aft.org/sites/default/files/release_bereavement121012.pdf. Difficulty concentrating was observed by 87 percent of teachers; withdrawal/disengagement and less class participation was observed by 82 percent; absenteeism observed by 72 percent; decrease in quality of work observed by 68 percent; less reliability in turning in assignments observed by 66 percent.

[24]Holly Torbic, "Children and Grief: But What About the Children?" *Home Healthcare Nurse* 29, no. 2 (2011): 67-79.

[25]Roberta L. Woodgate, "Sibling's Experiences with Childhood Cancer: A Different Way of Being in the Family," *Cancer Nursing* 29 (2006): 406-14.

[26]Eleanor Porteous, Elizabeth R. Peterson, and Claire Cartwright, "Siblings of Young People with Cancer in NZ: Experiences that Positively and Negatively Support Well-Being," *Journal of Pediatric Oncology Nursing* 36, no. 2 (2019): 119-30.

[27]David J. Schonfeld and Marcia Quackenbush, "After a Loved One Dies: How Children Grieve" (New York: New York Life Foundation, 2009), 10. Interestingly, parents have many of these same feelings—guilt, anger, confusion, or feeling needy (13).

[28]"Grieving in Schools."

[29]David A. Walters, "Grief and Loss: Towards an Existential Phenomenology of Child Spirituality," *International Journal of Children's Spirituality* 13, no. 3 (August 2008): 277.

[30]Alan D. Wolfelt, *A Child's View of Grief* (Fort Collins, CO: Companion, 2004), 3.

Wolfelt says grief is what people think and feel inside after someone they love dies, whereas mourning is the outward expression of our grief. Mourning is the "normal, healthy process of embracing the mystery of the death of someone loved."[31] Mourning can include, for example, crying, talking to other people about the death, sharing stories, putting together photo albums, and journaling.

Mourning is unsurprisingly a spiritual enterprise. We recognize this truism in the key relationships we use to define children's spirituality: the child-self relationship, the child-others relationship, and the child-God relationship. When a child loses a parent or a sibling, the child in some manner begins to ask child-self questions: "Who am I now that I do not have a mother (or father)? Who am I if I am not a sister (or brother) anymore? If I am not the middle brother (or sister) anymore?"

Child-others questions also arise: "How will others see me now? Will they think I am different? *Am* I different? Will they think I am weird?" And the child may ask child-God questions (even if the family is non-religious), including: "How could God let this happen? Why didn't God stop it? Was he just not paying attention? Why didn't God heal him? Where is Daddy now? Is he with God?"[32]

At some level, children also begin the process of making meaning of their loss, asking questions such as: "How could something this unfair happen? How can I go on if I will never get to see this person again? Who wants to live in a world where this can occur? What will become of our family now that this person is gone?"[33]

On a Sunday afternoon, seven-year-old Emily and her dad visited Emily's mother in the hospital for the last time. Emily's mother had been

---

[31]"About Dr. Alan Wolfelt," Center for Loss and Life Transition, www.centerforloss.com/about-the-center-for-loss/about-dr-alan-wolfelt. Accessed Feb. 16, 2021.

[32]The child's age and developmental stage will impact the types of questions he or she asks, according to Elaine Champagne, "Living and Dying: A Window on (Christian) Children's Spirituality," *International Journal of Children's Spirituality* 13, no. 3 (August 2008): 253-63. Champagne notes that various concepts are involved in children's understanding of death, and these understandings evolve according to their cognitive development and life experience. These concepts about death include universality (all will eventually die), irreversibility (e.g., a parent will not come back to life), and finality (nonfunctionality; parent cannot eat, talk, think, etc.).

[33]Schonfeld and Quackenbush, "After a Loved One Dies," 6.

sick for several months, and on that Sunday, she looked very small in the bed; her arms were thin, her hair was thin, and her face was thin. When Emily and her dad got home, Emily asked, "Is Mommy going to die?"

Her dad picked her up, sat down with her on his lap, and said, "Yes, Emily, Mommy is very sick, and the doctors think Mommy will die very soon."

Emily leaned against her dad's chest and was very quiet. After a few minutes her dad said, "Do you have any questions you want to ask me?"

In a whisper, Emily asked, "Will it hurt?"

When her dad had responded, Emily asked several more questions: "Where will she go when she dies? What will happen to her body? Why couldn't the doctors fix her? Will I still be able to talk to her?"

And last, Emily looked into her father's face and asked the most important question of all: "Will she still be my mother, even if she isn't here?"

Her dad tilted her chin up so he could look directly into her eyes, and said, "Yes, Emily. She will always be your mother."

SPIRITUALLY NURTURING CHILDREN
WHO HAVE LOST A PARENT OR SIBLING

Much of the literature regarding how to support children who have lost a parent or sibling is written for family members or helping professionals. Most teachers, children's ministers, and childcare workers are keenly aware that stepping into this most sensitive grieving place is presumptuous, perhaps even inappropriate.

However, as many of the accounts in this book illustrate, children will often lean into opportunities to grapple with their grief and loss when spiritually sensitive activities are available to them, such as walking a labyrinth, reading a thoughtful children's book, or hearing a Godly Play story.

Recently, in a course on nurturing spiritual development in children, my students and I had the opportunity to spend time with children whose parents were incarcerated. During the various times with the children, we read books together, wrote letters to God, shared our lives and stories, walked a labyrinth, and participated in two Godly Play stories.

One of the children was eleven-year-old Ella, the oldest of three daughters. Ella's dad had died a year earlier and her mother was in prison; she and her sisters were living with family friends. Carly, the student who spent the most time with Ella, wrote this in her final report:

> Over the semester, I noticed that Ella carries around guilt and shame for what has happened to her mom and dad. During one of our times together we had the opportunity to listen to the Godly Play Good Shepherd story. At the end of this story, her unprompted response was, "I want to be the Good Shepherd for my mom and sisters." While this is a pure desire, it is not a task that an eleven-year-old would usually place on herself. However, her response illustrates a side of Ella that she doesn't always know how to express. Godly Play gave us the chance to explore these deep-rooted feelings and emotions that she didn't even realize she had. Entering this Godly Play story enabled Ella (and me) to make the connection of her wanting to be the Good Shepherd for her family and me being able to tell her that there is another Good Shepherd who is watching over her too.

The Good Shepherd Godly Play story gave Ella a chance to wonder about and contemplate the things already going on in her heart—specifically, that with the death of her father and the absence of her mother, she felt responsible for her younger sisters.

One area that much of the literature says is generally neglected is providing a safe place for children to express their emotions. "Kids will have a wide range of reactions, just as adults do, from sadness to anger to rage to confusion and relief," says Kate Jackson.[34] Children may not talk about their feelings because they tend to take their cues from the adults around them, and adults may not state explicitly how they are feeling in order to shield their children from their grief. The children may thus infer that talking about the death is wrong or hurtful. Or they may fear that bringing up the subject will create even more sadness and more tears.[35]

When Riley's younger brother died, her second grade teacher asked her almost every day, "How are you today, Riley?"

---

[34] Kate Jackson, "How Children Grieve: Persistent Myths May Stand in the Way of Appropriate Care and Support for Children," *Social Work Today* 15, no. 2 (March/April 2015): 20.
[35] Jackson, "How Children Grieve."

Sometimes Riley would say, "I cried last night." Other days she would say, "I am sad," or "I am lonely."

And then one day Riley said, "My brother talked to me last night; he said he is okay."

Her teacher said, "I am so glad."

Riley said, "Me too."

Having a safe place to say how they are feeling helps children listen to their inner voice and connect with someone else—both important parts of children's spirituality.

A book that deals with parental death explicitly is *Missing Mommy* by Rebecca Cobb. It begins, "Some time ago, we said good-bye to Mommy. I am not sure where she has gone."[36] This simple, touching book explores emotions a grieving child may experience, including anger, guilt, sadness, and disorientation. It offers several opportunities that could nurture the child-self, child-others, and child-God relationships; it also provides ways to foster conversations that help a child make meaning and lean into hope.

A few years ago, Derrick, a father of three, died in a drowning accident. The suddenness and trauma of the event seemed to overwhelm everyone involved: his wife, their children, the church, the community. The evening before the memorial service, the family gathered for the visitation, as is common, to receive the comfort and support of those who knew their dad and husband. Extended family, church members, and work colleagues arrived wearing somber clothing and stoic faces. Guest after guest tenderly hugged the children, aged ten, thirteen, and sixteen, and their mom, murmuring in muted voices, "I'm so sorry." Then they sat quietly around the room in the provided chairs speaking softly to each other. The sixteen-year-old, Cory, a boy with Down syndrome, began to exhibit distress, and as the evening wore on, he became more and more agitated.

Suddenly, Cory stood up and announced in a loud voice, "I'm sad!" He paused, then said in an even louder voice: *"I am just really, really sad!"*

---

[36]Rebecca Cobb, *Missing Mommy: A Book About Bereavement* (New York: Puffin Books, 2013), 4-5.

There was a hush over the room as everyone stared at Cory. Then Cory's uncle, Derrick's brother, stood, walked over to Cory, put his arm around his shoulder, and said, "Cory, we are too. We are all just really, really sad."

Cory, less aware of social norms in such a setting, expressed loudly what everyone else was feeling, and his straightforward simple words gave permission for everyone else to acknowledge their deep sorrow as well. And Derrick's sensitive, empathetic remark offered validation and support for Cory's feelings.

GRIEF AND LOSS, CHILDREN'S SPIRITUALITY, AND RESILIENCE

Children whose parents are divorcing, children who are seriously ill, and children who have lost a parent or sibling to death are all dealing with severe grief and loss. An important part of the grieving process is the recognition that it is a process that often lasts a lifetime. Children need not be rushed through so things can return to normal. Preadolescent and younger children tend to grieve cyclically—that is, they will ask questions over and over, then go out and ride their bike or play with their dolls, then a few days later spend an hour sobbing with grief, then immediately go back to playing. Their grief may not be like adults' grief.[37]

Realizing that grief is not a problem for adults to help children "fix" or "solve" or even "get over"[38] can allow adults to give children the time they need to adjust to new realities after a divorce, during an illness, or after losing a parent or sibling. Grieving and mourning after any of these losses includes learning to cope with emotions and other changes resulting from loss, developing new types of relationships that emerge after a divorce or a death, finding meaning from the experience of loss, and absorbing the experience into their lives.[39]

Crawford, Wright, and Masten write, "We know that suffering and adversity are spiritual concerns, and our understanding of what will

---

[37]Torbic, "Children and Grief."
[38]Jackson, "How Children Grieve," 20.
[39]Jackson, "How Children Grieve."

foster resilience will be more comprehensive when we incorporate 'spir- itual' processes into [other supportive] approaches" such as counseling and therapy.[40] Activities we have discussed in this chapter and throughout the book that can be seen as spiritual processes include reading children's books, walking a labyrinth, asking wondering questions, telling Godly Play stories, and providing time and space for quietness; these activities foster those relationships that are integral to spirituality—the child-self, child-others, child-God relationships—and as we know, these relation- ships encourage resilience.

---

[40]Crawford, Wright, and Masten, "Resilience and Spirituality," 367.

CHAPTER TWELVE

Good Books

Good stories . . . return our attention continually
to the contemplation of issues of the soul.

DARLENE L. WITTE-TOWNSEND AND EMILY DIGUILIO

WHEN CHILDREN COME FACE TO FACE with severe adversity, they sometimes contend with the reality of death, the need for meaning, and the experience of aloneness.[1] And good children's books offer surprising venues to begin to tap into these existential spiritual realms. The imaginative worlds of fables, fairy tales, animal stories, nursery rhymes, and other children's stories create inherent opportunities to nurture children's relationships with self, others, and God (as they understand God). This chapter shares thoughtful, reflective ways to foster these spiritual discussions and illustrates the process with several books.

HOW BOOKS CAN PROMPT EASY AND NATURAL CONVERSATIONS

As long as I have known Emma, now a teenager, she has exhibited a somewhat wily bent. Even as a preschooler she was quite precocious interpersonally, with a surprising way of perceiving weaknesses in others and using those insights to her advantage. This quality is somewhat disconcerting to see in a child, and when she was about six years old, I read

---

[1] Jerome W. Berryman, *Teaching Godly Play: How to Mentor the Spiritual Development of Children*, 2nd ed. (Denver: Morehouse Education Resources, 2009).

her *Anansi and the Moss-Covered Rock*,[2] a book I have read with other children over the years.

Many West African stories feature Anansi, a fabled spider who loves to deceive those around him. This particular Anansi story depicts the spider tricking the other animals in the jungle out of their food supplies with a magic rock. Anansi tricks a lion, an elephant, a giraffe, a hippo, a zebra, and others. While the trickery is going on, Little Bush Deer is peering from behind the bushes observing Anansi's shenanigans and the plight of the other animals. Little Bush Deer decides to get the food back for all the animals, and she does so by turning Anansi's magic trick back on himself. Little Bush Deer returns the food to the animals and all is well.

After I read this book to Emma, I asked her, "Who are you in this story?" Usually when I read this book to children, they say they are the Little Bush Deer—because children want to be the hero, I suppose.

But when I asked Emma this question, she paused, then responded with glee, "I am the spider!"

Actually, I wasn't surprised. But I was curious about how she would respond to the second question: "Why are you the spider?"

Emma replied, "Because I like to trick people!"

I was indeed already cognizant of this quality in Emma, but I didn't know she was so keenly aware of it, nor did I guess she would so transparently admit it to me.

Emma then added, "But I'm the Little Bush Deer too."

"Why are you the Little Bush Deer?"

"Because I like to spy on people!"

Such a surprising and revelatory conversation!

Child-others relationships. When I read a book to a child (even a child as young as two or three), I usually ask them who they are in the story and why, as I did with Emma. Doing so offers an opportunity for me to see into the heart of the child. Interestingly, some children also ask me, "Who are you in the story?" And when I choose a character and tell the child why, they see into my heart as well. Asking these two questions

---

[2]Eric Kimmel, *Anansi and the Moss-Covered Rock* (New York: Holiday House, 1990).

is one powerful way to foster the child-others relationship that is so important to a child's spiritual growth and development.

Another question that may trigger interpersonal insights is, "What is your favorite page in this book?" Once the child finds the page, the reader may ask, "What is special about this page?" or "What do you like about this page?" Again, seeing through the eyes of the child what gave them pleasure, what caused them to wonder, or what prompted feelings of empathy, fear, hope, or courage can also open the heart of the child to the reader. Of course, the child may eventually ask the reader, "What is your favorite page?" And again, the child will hear the reader's heart, further cultivating that child-others relationship.

Reading aloud to a group of children adds another dimension to the self-others aspect of spirituality: "It is here in the silence, waiting together at the end of a story that the read-aloud experience is transformation. It becomes a place of transcendence where the child-as-listener-alone becomes the child-as-listener-with-others. A connection is made there in the silence."[3] Fostering this sense of connection is crucial in children; it is difficult for them to develop a conscience, realize their need for community, or find their place in the world if this self-other connectedness has not been awakened.[4]

An important piece of the child-others relationship is empathy—the ability to understand and share the feelings of another person. A recent book that powerfully elicits a sense of responsiveness to the other is *Each Kindness* by Jacqueline Woodson. (See the end of the chapter for a bibliography that includes this and other books discussed here.) When a new girl, Maya, arrives in Chloe's class, Chloe and her friends do not include Maya in their play, and they turn away when Maya invites them to join her with her new set of jacks. What is unique about this book is that it is written in the first-person voice of Chloe, who is both a bully in the story and a bystander as others bully. Later, when Maya's family moves away, Chloe reconsiders the missed opportunity to show kindness, and the book closes as Chloe plaintively expresses regret.

---

[3]Darlene L. Witte-Townsend and Emily DiGuilio, "Something from Nothing: Exploring Dimensions of Children's Knowing through the Repeated Reading of Favorite Books," *International Journal of Children's Spirituality* 9, no. 2 (2004): 134.
[4]Witte-Townsend and DiGuilio, "Something from Nothing," 135.

Other books that can foster that most wonderful quality of otherness are *Those Shoes* by Maribeth Boelts, *Rainbow Fish* and *Rainbow Fish to the Rescue* by Marcus Pfister, *Eugene the Brave* by Ellen Conford, and *Last Stop on Market Street* by Matt de la Peña. Somewhat older children will enjoy *A Lighthouse Family Treasury: The Storm; The Whale; The Eagle; The Turtle* by Cynthia Rylant.

Child-self relationship. Other insights may also be revealed during moments of discussion surrounding the reading of good children's books. When children talk about themselves as a character in the book, they may begin to see things in themselves they had not realized before. I do not know if Emma had ever discussed her "sneaky" qualities with anyone, or if she had ever even acknowledged them to herself. But conversations that tap into child-others relationships are good vehicles for the child-self relationship to be enhanced as well.

Some books are particularly well-suited to helping us find ourselves in our questions while we ask them.[5] Two such books are *Something from Nothing* by Phoebe Gilman and *Joseph Had a Little Overcoat* by Simms Taback, similar retellings of a Yiddish folk tale. In *Something from Nothing*, a grandfather makes a garment for his grandson; eventually the little boy outgrows the garment and the grandfather creates another use from it—a jacket, a vest, a scarf, a tie, which then become ragged or stained. Last, there is just enough material for the grandfather to make a covered button. When the boy loses the button, nothing else can be made. But the boy decides, "There is just enough material here to make . . . a wonderful story," and proceeds to write down this story.

Both *Something from Nothing* and *Joseph Had a Little Overcoat* capture the truisms that life changes, we experience material losses, and relationships help us cope with changes and losses. Further, in these stories, Joseph takes up the challenge to make something from nothing. That same question—"Who are you in the story?"—offers the opportunity for the child to consider how he or she is like the grandfather or like Joseph and to consider how the child handles the problem of lost, broken, or unusable possessions, a question that can prompt self-examination.

---

[5] Witte-Townsend and DiGuilio, "Something from Nothing."

Other children's books I have found that foster relaxed interpersonal conversation and perhaps intrapersonal understanding include *A Splendid Friend Indeed*, one of Suzanne Bloom's Goose and Bear stories, *The Runaway Bunny* by Margaret Wise Brown, and *Frederick* by Leo Lionni.

CHILDREN'S LITERATURE

Besides encouraging good conversations, building trust, promoting self-understanding, and fostering empathy and interpersonal connection, sharing good literature can help children:

- Hope
- Transcend hard conditions
- Glimpse deeper realities
- Come to know the beauty of goodness
- Recognize love
- Experience joy and peace
- Confront or cope with their fear of evil[6]

Children seek out adults to help them name feelings and experiences and to make sense out of what happens in their lives. Reading children's books together creates natural opportunities to accompany children in these identifying and meaning-making processes.

CHILDREN'S BOOKS AND RESILIENCE

Mandy, a friend who lives in Oklahoma, adopted a little girl from China a few years ago. This child was born with an unformed hand and lived in an orphanage in China her first two years of life. In those two years she experienced the loss of her birth parents, placement in an orphanage that met her basic needs but little more, and adoption into a new family with a new language and a new country. Since that time she has also had to contend with ongoing comments and stares from children and others

---

[6]Sue Kendall, "The Role of Picture Books in Children's Spiritual Development and Meaning Making," *International Journal of Children's Spirituality* 4, no. 1 (1999): 61-76; Barbara K. Myers and Michal E. Myers, "Engaging Children's Spirit and Spirituality Through Literature," *Childhood Education* 76, no. 1 (1999): 28-32; Witte-Townsend and DiGuilio, "Something from Nothing."

about her "lucky fin," which is what she and her adoptive family call her special hand.[7]

Mandy has blogged often about the attachment and bonding issues the family has experienced. She wrote a beautiful post in 2015 describing several books that have encouraged the growing attachment their daughter is experiencing. Here is an excerpt from that blog:

Before my daughter understood or spoke much English, we made a picture book of us doing nurturing and fun activities with our daughter (recommended in the book *Attaching in Adoption* by Deborah Gray). Every photo was of us together. Our daughter was resistant to nurture for many months, so we had to get creative with the photos we included. One page in the book was a photo of me putting a Band-Aid on her "owie"; one page was of my daughter asleep in my husband's arms; another was a photo of me pushing her in a swing; and another was of me feeding her Gummy Bears (her personal favorite). Many times throughout the day and during high-anxiety moments, my daughter would reach for this book. This simple book was a reminder to her that we are fun and we take care of her. We made several copies of this book for just a few dollars at our local drugstore's photo development center.

One of my daughter's favorite books is *My Mommy* from the Disney Baby Animal Stories [twelve-book set]. Although the book is very simple and small, it was a helpful tool to help her understand that I will take care of her. The words in the book have become a powerful script my daughter recites daily. "My mommy feeds me," "My mommy keeps me safe and warm," and "My mommy loves to cuddle" are the phrases I will hear her recite several times per day. When my daughter was resistant to nurture, we turned what we saw in the book into a time to play: this was a great opportunity to demonstrate nurture with play.

Mommy Hugs by Anne Gutman and Georg Hallensleben is another favorite. We read this book each night at bedtime, and my daughter loves to act it out with me. The book shows different mommy animals hugging their baby animal and ends with a human mother and child hugging. Each

---

[7]In the movie *Finding Nemo*, the title character calls his slightly smaller fin his "lucky fin"; since then families with children who have a finger or hand abnormality have tended to call the special appendage a lucky fin.

time I hug her the way the mommy animal does, my daughter responds affectionately and says, "Oh, that's so sweet."[8]

Mandy also recommends books by Cindy R. Lee that address issues adopted children (and others) may encounter. These books specifically reflect Karyn Purvis's recommendations in *The Connected Child*;[9] each one teaches an important trust-based intervention concept or script from Purvis's well-known work with children from hard places. For example, *Baby Owl Lost Her Whoo* tells the story of a baby owl who was "left alone" and needs a mommy owl to show the baby owl what is best. According to Moore:

> This book gives me a gentle and playful way to engage and correct my daughter. For example, when my daughter cries and demands that she wants a cookie for breakfast and says, "Gimme a cookie right now!" I might say, "Whoa, precious baby owl! Who is the mommy owl?" and I recite the line from the book about the mommy owl making sure the baby owl eats healthy food. Usually, this has helped my daughter even in the moment when it is hard to accept "no," because let's be honest, I also want a cookie for breakfast.[10]

Other books that build trust and offer assurance are *Mama, Do You Love Me?* and *Papa, Do You Love Me?* by Barbara Joosse, *The Invisible String* by Patrice Harst, and *The Kissing Hand* by Audrey Penn.

For children who have experienced trauma, grief, or loss, reading books such as those noted above can help rebuild that foundational psychosocial quality of trust, and building trust is a requisite part of resilience.

CONCLUSION

The conversation with Emma outlined at the beginning of this chapter gave me courage to address a specific issue that had been emerging in Emma over a couple of years: she loved to annoy, trick, exasperate,

---

[8]Mandy Moore, "How Children's Books Helped My Family," No Hands but Ours (blog), March 1, 2015, www.facebook.com/NoHandsButOurs. Used by permission.
[9]Karyn Purvis, David R. Cross, and Wendy Lyons Sunshine, *The Connected Child: Bring Hope and Healing to Your Adoptive Family* (New York: McGraw-Hill, 2007).
[10]Moore, "How Children's Books Helped."

aggravate, and taunt her little brother, Lucas. In general, she had been making his life miserable for some time. So when Emma came to visit us for a few days when she was eight, we began a conversation that built on the openness she had displayed when we read the Anansi book.

"How are things going with Lucas?"

Emma paused, then spoke in a loud, irritated, and dramatic voice: "It's *war!*"

"Do you want it to be war?"

Pause. "Not really."

"Is there anything you can do?"

Another pause. "I don't know."

"Do you think you have a soft heart toward your brother?"

"Not really."

"Do you have a hard heart toward your brother?"

"I think so."

"Is there anything we can do about that?"

Long sigh. "I don't think so."

"Do you think we can pray about it?"

"I guess so, but I don't think it will do any good."

We did pray about it, every night she was with us.

Not long after this, Lucas spent a few days with us, and we talked a bit about his relationship with Emma. He didn't really want to pray about her (either), so I asked him what he would say to God if he wanted to talk to God about her. He said, "I would ask him why did he stick me with a sister like her."

A bit of hardheartedness here too.

Over the next several years, these deep, relational conversations that began in their preschool years as we read books together continued. When Emma and Lucas were twelve and ten years old, their mother developed a chronic illness that has been challenging for the family.

The last time we discussed their relationship was when Emma was fourteen and Lucas was twelve, and this time both children were present. I asked, "How are things between you two now? I know you used to have some troubles with each other."

They looked at each other, and a slow smile began to appear on both of their faces. Lucas spoke first: "Oh, I like Sissy now. We get along pretty good."

Emma agreed: "Yeah, it's all good."

I asked, "What has made the difference?"

Emma gave me a serious look. "Well, we have to help out a lot more now, with chores and stuff, you know, since Mama's been sick. We don't have time to mess with each other."

Reading books with Emma and Lucas over many years nurtured my relationship with both of these children and theirs with each other; it provided the fertile ground for some wonderful conversations; and it eventually contributed to the resilience the children have exhibited as their family has dealt with an ongoing challenging situation.

CHILDREN'S BOOKS REFERENCED IN THIS CHAPTER

Bloom, Suzanne. *A Splendid Friend Indeed*. Honesdale, PA: Boyds Mills Press, 2009.

Boelts, Maribeth. *Those Shoes*. Illustrated by Nora Z. Jones. Sommerville, MA: Candlewick, 2009.

Brown, Margaret Wise. *The Runaway Bunny*. Illustrated by Clement Hurd. New York: HarperFestival, 2017 (originally published 1942).

Conford, Ellen. *Eugene the Brave*. Illustrated by John Larrecq. Boston: Little, Brown, 1978.

de la Peña, Matt. *Last Stop on Market Street*. Illustrated by Christian Robinson. New York: G. P. Putnam's Sons, 2015.

Gilman, Phoebe. *Something from Nothing*. New York: Scholastic, 1992.

Gutman, Anne, and Georg Hallensleben. *Daddy Cuddles*. Illustrated by Sara Acton. San Francisco: Chronicle Books, 2005.

Gutman, Anne, and Georg Hallensleben. *Daddy Kisses*. Illustrated by Georg Hallensleben. San Francisco: Chronicle Books, 2003.

Gutman, Anne, and Georg Hallensleben. *Mommy Hugs*. Illustrated by Georg Hallensleben. San Francisco: Chronicle Books, 2003.

Harst, Patrice. *The Invisible String*. Illustrated by Geoff Stevenson. Camarillo, CA: Devorss, 2000.

Joosse, Barbara. *Mama, Do You Love Me?* Illustrated by Barbara Lavalle. San Francisco: Chronicle Books, 1998.

Joosse, Barbara. *Papa, Do You Love Me?* Illustrated by Barbara Lavallee. San Francisco: Chronicle Books, 2005.

Lee, Cindy R. *Baby Owl Lost Her Whoo*. Scotts Valley, CA: CreateSpace, 2014.

Lionni, Leo. *Frederick*. New York: Weekly Reader, 1967.

Penn, Audrey. *The Kissing Hand*. Illustrated by Ruth Harper. Indianapolis, IN: Tanglewood, 1993.

Pfister, Marcus. *Rainbow Fish*. New York: NorthSouth Books, 1999.

Pfister, Marcus. *Rainbow Fish to the Rescue*. New York: NorthSouth Books, 1999.

Rylant, Cynthia. *A Lighthouse Family Treasury: The Storm; The Whale; The Eagle; The Turtle*. Illustrated by Preston McDaniels. San Diego, CA: Beach Lane Books, 2016.

Taback, Simms. *Joseph Had a Little Overcoat*. New York: Viking-Penguin, 1999.

Woodson, Jacqueline. *Each Kindness*. Illustrated by E. B. Lewis. New York: Nancy Paulsen Books, 2012.

OTHER RECOMMENDED CHILDREN'S BOOKS

Below I have listed books recommended by colleagues that offer opportunities to enhance the child-self relationship, the child-others relationship, and the child-God relationship. These books also help children make meaning, cope with losses, and find hope—all processes that contribute to resilience. The commentary is provided by the following:

- Dana Kennamer, PhD, associate dean of the College of Education and Human Services and the chair of the Department of Teacher Education at Abilene Christian University, Abilene, Texas.

- Mimi Larson, PhD, visiting assistant professor of Christian formation and ministry at Wheaton College, Wheaton, Illinois, and adjunct assistant professor of educational studies at Trinity Evangelical Divinity School, Deerfield, Illinois.

- Trevecca Okholm, MA, adjunct professor of practical theology at Azusa Pacific University, Azusa, California.

- Robin Turner, DMin, director of Parent's Day Out at St. Augustine's Episcopal Church in Oak Cliff, Dallas, Texas.

Coles, Robert. *The Story of Ruby Bridges*. Special anniversary ed. Illustrated by George Ford. New York: Scholastic Paperbacks, 2010. The story of brave, six-year-old Ruby who integrated schools in New Orleans in 1960, exhibiting resilience and courage. (Trevecca Okholm)

DePaolo, Tomie. *Now One Foot, Now the Other*. New York: Puffin, 2006. A grandfather teaches a little boy to walk and then the little boy helps the grandfather walk again after a stroke. (Dana Kennamer)

Fox, Mem. *Wilfrid Gordon McDonald Partridge*. Illustrated by Julie Vivas. La Jolla, CA:

Kane Miller, 1989. A little boy wants to understand what it means when an older adult has lost her memory. (Dana Kennamer)

Fleming, Virginia. *Be Good to Eddie Lee*. Illustrated by Floyd Cooper. New York: Puffin, 1997. Helps children feel others' experiences, in this case, a child with Down syndrome. (Dana Kennamer)

Grimes, Nikki. *The Watcher*. Illustrated by Bryan Collier. Grand Rapids, MI: Eerdmans Books for Young Readers, 2017. Based on Psalm 121. (Dana Kennamer)

Henkes, Kevin. *Wemberly Worried*. New York: Greenwillow Books, 2010. For children who worry. (Dana Kennamer)

Karst, Patrice. *The Invisible String*. Illustrated by Geoff Stevenson. Camarillo, CA: Devorss, 2000. On overcoming the fear of loneliness or separation. (Trevecca Okholm)

Kuntz, Doug, and Amy Shrodes. *Lost and Found Cat: The True Story of Kunkush's Incredible Journey*. Illustrated by Sue Cornelison. New York: Crown Books for Young Readers, 2017. Iraq refugee family flees Mosul exhibiting resilience in the face of loss. (Trevecca Okholm)

Lai, Thanhhà. *Inside Out and Back Again*. New York: HarperCollins, 2013. A book about a ten-year-old's experience leaving war-torn Saigon and immigrating to rural Alabama in 1975; helps children understand how we come across to those from other cultures. (Mimi Larson)

Lord, Betty Bao. *In the Year of the Boar and Jackie Robinson*. Illustrated by Marc Simont. New York: HarperCollins, 2019 (originally published 1984). On empathy for other perspectives. (Robin Turner and Mimi Larson)

Ladwig, Tim. *Psalm 23*. Grand Rapids, MI: Eerdmans Books for Young Readers, 1997. Beautifully illustrated version set in the inner city. (Dana Kennamer)

Ludwig, Trudy. *The Invisible Boy*. Illustrated by Patrice Barton. New York: Knopf Books for Young Readers, 2013. About a little boy everyone ignores who sees the new child and welcomes him. (Dana Kennamer)

McCarney, Rosemary. *Where Will I Live?* Toronto, ON: Second Story Press, 2017. Helps children feel others' experiences, in this case, refugee children from all around the world. (Dana Kennamer)

Oberthür, Rainer. *Our Father*. Illustrated by Barbara Nascimben. Grand Rapids, MI: Eerdmans Books for Young Readers, 2016. Based on the Lord's Prayer. (Dana Kennamer)

Park, Linda Sue. *A Long Walk to Water*. Illustrated by Brian Pinkney, HMH Books for Young Readers, 2011. Two Sudanese children exhibit resilience and hope. (Trevecca Okholm)

Paterson, Katherine. *Bridge to Terabithia*. Illustrated by Donna Diamond. New York: HarperCollins, 2017 (originally published 1987). About friendship across socioeconomic lines and empathy in loss. (Robin Turner)

Paterson, Katherine. *The Great Gilly Hopkins*. New York: HarperCollins, 2004 (originally published 1987). On building empathy for someone in foster care and building trust with caretakers. (Robin Turner)

Recorvits, Helen. *My Name is Yoon*. Illustrated by Gabi Swiatkowska. New York: Square Fish, 2014. Helps children feel others' experiences, in this case, a child coming to the United States from Korea. (Dana Kennamer)

Robinson, Barbara. *The Best Christmas Pageant Ever*. Illustrated by Lauren Cornell. New York: HarperCollins, 2011. Empathy for people navigating hidden rules. (Robin Turner)

Woodson, Jacqueline. *Visiting Day*. Illustrated by James Ransome. New York: Puffin Books, 2015. Helps children feel others' experiences, in this case, a little girl who visits her father in prison. (Dana Kennamer)

PART FIVE

In Conclusion

CHAPTER THIRTEEN

Hope and Resilience

Hope is the thing with feathers, that perches in the soul,
and sings the tune without the words and never stops at all.

EMILY DICKINSON

I BEGAN CHAPTER ONE with the story of our three-month-old grandson who became critically ill. For several heart-stopping hours, doctors, medical technicians, and nurses performed intervention after intervention to keep his lungs working, stabilize his blood pressure, and regulate his heart rate, oxygen, and carbon dioxide levels. Then when he seemed to be moving out of immediate danger, a CT scan showed evidence of a brain bleed and consequent brain damage.

We were heartbroken. The doctors sedated Roham with a fentanyl drip, and for three days we awaited an opportunity for an MRI to determine the extent of the brain damage. Because of Roham's fragile condition, it was difficult to regulate his vitals long enough to get a full scan; finally, on day four the MRI was completed, but results were not available until the next day. On day five, we began watching for signs that Roham was coming out of the fentanyl-induced sleep, hoping he would be present with us.

I was alone with Roham for a couple of hours that afternoon. I began singing over him as he lay still, attached to an array of tubes and wires feeding him, monitoring his heart, helping him breathe, administering medication. As I sang, in one small movement, Roham turned his head, opened his eyes, and looked directly at me.

I continued to sing. He stared for a few more seconds, then closed his eyes and turned his head back. He was in there. Though the test results had not come back yet, I could see that Roham was there: he saw me, he heard me, he connected with me.

An hour later the MRI results came back. No brain damage was detectable.

And Roham began to recover.

When Roham was nine months old, our daughter asked someone to photograph her family at a local park. Our Christmas present that year was an album of these wonderful photos. And on page four was a solo picture of Roham. It is captioned, "The boy who lived."

This story will be told over and over in Roham's lifetime; he is the boy who lived. When all hope seemed lost, we did not give up. We sang over him and waited with hope for the signs of life. Today he is surrounded by people who love him, hold him, listen to his stories, tell him about God, share their stories of hope and life, read him books, and share their hearts, their struggles, and their hopes. They (and we) will help him make sense of the hard things he will face.

Resilient people who have survived a variety of adversities often identify hope and finding meaning as healing influences in their lives.[1] Children in hard places need hope, and they need the people around them to have hope as well.

As I write this chapter, the coronavirus pandemic is raging around the world. In the fall of 2020, Lipscomb University, where I teach, welcomed a freshman class that had been deeply impacted by the pandemic. These students completed their senior year of high school far differently from the way they had envisioned it: they concluded the year online, at home with parents, or perhaps not at all, really. Furthermore, some students' parents lost their jobs; some lost a grandparent to Covid-19; some lost summer jobs; all were impacted by the social distancing guidelines that closed malls, restaurants, sporting events, and churches. These seventeen-, eighteen-, and nineteen-year-old students came to Lipscomb

---

[1]Ann Masten, *Ordinary Magic: Resilience in Development* (New York: Guilford Press, 2015).

University during a serious economic recession. By helping them lean into their already existing protective factors—their families, other supportive relationships, their self-efficacy, and especially their spiritual resources—we have been promoting a resilient mindset that will carry them through their college years and into adulthood.

For many young people, this pandemic with its accompanying fears, limitations, strictures, and losses has been the first serious threat they have faced. As mentioned in chapter eleven, Jerome Berryman came to believe that children and adolescents dealing with hardship grapple with existential limits such as death, the threat of freedom, aloneness, and the need for meaning.[2] During this pandemic, the children and adolescents of Generation Z have peered into these limits—either consciously or unconsciously.

One key role for parents and those working with children and adolescents coping in this troubling season is to help them acquire language to address the concerns Berryman describes. Nurturing the relationships emphasized throughout this book—the child-self, child-others, and child-God relationships—provides a spiritual language that young people can use to articulate their fears as they make meaning, seek belonging, and lean into hope.[3]

Meaning making. The coronavirus pandemic will likely be the defining event of Generation Z. Helping the children, adolescents, and emerging adults of this generation begin to make meaning of the events of 2020 and beyond will contribute to their resilience. Vaclav Havel, the first president of the Czech Republic after the fall of communism in

---

[2]Jerome W. Berryman, *Teaching Godly Play: How to Mentor the Spiritual Development of Children,* 2nd ed. (Denver: Morehouse Education Resources, 2009), 46; Jerome W. Berryman, "The Chaplain's Strange Language: A Unique Contribution to the Health Care Team," in *Life, Faith, Hope, and Magic: The Chaplaincy in Pediatric Cancer Care,* ed. Jan van Eys and Edward J. Mahnke (Austin: University of Texas Press, 1985).

[3]Thema Bryant-Davis, Monica U. Ellis, Elizabeth Burke-Maynard, Nathan Moon, Pamela A. Counts, and Gera Anderson, "Religiosity, Spirituality, and Trauma Recovery in the Lives of Children and Adolescents," *Professional Psychology: Research and Practice* 43, no. 4 (2012): 306-14, citing Marie Good and Teena Willoughby, "Adolescence as a Sensitive Period for Spiritual Development," *Child Development Perspectives* 2 (2008): 32-37, and Mark D. Holder, Ben Coleman, and Judi M. Wallace, "Spirituality, Religiousness, and Happiness in Children Aged 8-12 Years," *Journal of Happiness Studies* 11 (2010): 131-50.

Eastern Europe, said, "Hope is not the conviction that something will turn out well, but the certainty that something makes sense, regardless of how it turns out."[4] It is incumbent on teachers, parents, and other leaders to intentionally walk with this younger generation as they (and we) seek understanding and make sense of a world where we acknowledge that the future will not look like the past, that science cannot always save us, and that unknowns lie before us—all the while leaning into the words of Julian of Norwich that "all shall be well, all shall be well, and all manner of thing[s] shall be well."[5]

A sense of belonging. This generation has shared an experience that will shape their outlook, their perspective, and their sense of reality for the rest of their lives as the 9/11 experience has shaped the Millennial generation. Older generations can aid this current generation in creating a sense of belonging with their peers who traversed similar losses, griefs, and fears of the coronavirus pandemic in parallel settings. Those in their sixties, seventies, eighties, and nineties can also be instrumental in inviting this younger generation to see similarities to previous generational experiences such as the Great Depression, World War II, the civil rights movement, and various financial crises of the 1980s, 2000s, and now again in the 2020s. Every generation faces some form of upheaval and loss, and this generation can take its place alongside those who have survived earlier crises, perhaps making connections that can contribute to their own resilience.

A sense of hope. Most important is to help this generation lean into hope—that is, to see into a different future, one that is not circumscribed by a virus but that lives more wisely in light of what we have learned from the events and circumstances of this current season.

Twenty-five years ago, I and my family were part of a church plant that grew from about twenty-five to around seven hundred people in four years. My husband was one of three lead pastors, and I was one of the children's ministers. Those were rich, fruitful, life-changing years for me,

---

[4]Vaclav Havel, *Disturbing the Peace* (New York: Knopf, 1990), 181.
[5]Julian of Norwich, *Revelations of Divine Love*, trans. Father John Julian (Brewseter, MA: Paraclete, 2011), 64.

my family, and many in the church; it was the most authentic, Spirit-filled fellowship we had ever experienced. Nevertheless, after four years, that beloved faith community broke up, leaving behind aching loss, intense grief, and searing pain. It was the hardest season my family has faced; our life simply fell down. I hardly functioned for a year. My children, who were eleven, thirteen, and nineteen at the time, were deeply affected by the church breakup, but they were even more distraught by the sense of hopelessness they saw in me.

During this time a verse memorized in childhood rose in my heart: "May the God of hope fill you with all joy and peace as you trust in him, so that you may overflow with hope by the power of the Holy Spirit" (Romans 15:13). I began to rehearse that verse several times a day in my mind, and sometimes I spoke the words aloud. I eventually began to live into them, to believe that God was at work in my heart, in the hearts of the others, restoring, redeeming, rebuilding the ruins. I found in those days of recovery that I needed hope as much as I needed air to breathe.

Resilience cannot flourish without hope.[6]

Everyone needs hope.

Children need hope. This includes:

- Children whose parents are incarcerated
- Children who did not make the drill team or the baseball team
- Children who failed fourth grade
- Children who are refugees
- Children facing chronic or terminal illness
- Children who are being bullied
- Children living in generational poverty
- Children who feel they are less because of their race or ethnicity
- Children who are rejected by a friend group
- Children who survived a school shooting
- Children with special needs

---

[6]David Crenshaw, "A Resilience Framework."

- Children whose parents are divorcing
- Children who are former child soldiers

Ishmael Beah was twelve years old when Sierra Leone's brutal, decade-long civil war reached his village in the 1990s. He was swept up into the army as a child soldier for three years. Beah was eventually rescued by a rehabilitation organization, with whom he spent eight months recovering from his experiences. Beah spent the next decade processing those experiences—the war, the drugs, the killings, the loss of his fellow soldiers, and his recovery from such trauma.[7]

In an interview, Beah was asked how he coped, how he survived, and what helped him recover in the aftermath.[8] Beah attributed his resilience to the intervention of adults who cared for him with compassion and kindness, who showed him he could trust himself again and that he could trust adults. He also spoke of his friend Saidu, who had simply given up and died as the boys were running and hiding from soldiers who wanted to recapture them. The interviewer asked Beah, "What was the difference between your outlook and Saidu's?" Beah responded:

> We had to have hope, regardless of how little it was. Even if it meant celebrating just having a chance to stop and drink clean water. Once you lose hope, you lose the determination to continue running, during the context of war. You are happy just to receive a loaf of bread because holding on to that hope gives you strength to live through the next thing.[9]

Over the past several decades, Bessel Van Der Kolk has worked with child and adult survivors of trauma,[10] and over those decades he has asked incoming patients, "Have you given up all hope of finding meaning in your life?" Among those who experienced major trauma

---

[7]Ishmael Beah, *A Long Way Home: Memoirs of a Boy Soldier* (New York: Sarah Crichton Books, 2007).

[8]Gina Stepp, "Ishmael Beah: Hope Springs Eternal," Vision, August 7, 2007, www.vision.org /interview-ishmael-beah-child-soldier-613.

[9]Stepp, "Ishmael Beah."

[10]Bessel Van Der Kolk is former codirector of the National Child Traumatic Stress Network, professor of psychiatry at Boston University School of Medicine, and president of the Trauma Research Foundation in Brookline, Massachusetts. His books include *Psychological Trauma*, 2nd ed. (Washington, DC: American Psychiatric Publishing, 2003), *Traumatic Stress* (New York: Guilford Press, 2006), and *The Body Keeps the Score* (New York: Penguin, 2015).

after age twenty, 10 percent answered "yes." Among those who experienced major trauma *prior to age five*, the figure was *74 percent*.[11] Clearly,
children's experiences of trauma often affects their hope and meaning
making later in life.

Resilience is integrally tied to hope, especially in children and adolescents. And hope is tied to a future—to the ability to push through the
present believing in a better future. God explicitly ties these ideas together in the well-known passage, "'For I know the plans I have for you,'
declares the LORD, 'plans to prosper you and not to harm you, plans to
give you hope and a future'" (Jeremiah 29:11). Coming to see oneself as
a child of God, learning to connect with others, and believing in a God
who is present, who sees, who cares, and who weeps with us can be the
anchor of hope that we and the children we serve need.

And as we walk with children on their spiritual journeys, we can
embody that hope for them and with them. So when a child looks at
you with heart-rending sadness and says, "I don't know if I believe in
God anymore," you can say, "Then I will believe for you until you can
believe again."

And when a child says, "This hurts too much; I just hurt, and hurt, and
hurt. Won't it ever go away?" you can say, "It does hurt, but it will not
always be so. You will not always hurt like you do today."

"Do you really think so?" the child may respond.

And you can say, "I *know* so."

Most of us will not spend time with children who have survived a
school shooting or life as a child soldier; nevertheless, it is very likely
that we will come to know children who have encountered racial epi-
thets, who are chronically or terminally ill, who have been bullied, who
have lived in generational poverty, or who have lost a sibling or parent
to death.

Unless we are counselors or therapists, we will not be the child's
primary mentor. However, these children are in our classrooms, in our
afterschool programs, in our neighborhoods, and in our children's

---

[11]As reported in James Garbarino and Claire Bedard, "Spiritual Challenges to Children Facing
Violent Trauma," *Childhood* 3, no. 4 (1996): 470.

ministries. They may be our own children or grandchildren, our nieces or nephews.

In our lives, as we have opportunity, we can help construct with the children a bridge from their already existing spirituality to the actual experiences of their lives, believing as we do (and as research supports) that this connection in ineffable ways generates resilience.

Epilogue

I WILL CLOSE THIS BOOK by rejoining the story in the introduction about Ruth Walker and her children who survived Hurricane Katrina in New Orleans.

The Walker family lost their apartment and most of their personal belongings; the children left their friends, their schools, and their dad. Ruth left her job, her friends, her life in New Orleans. They experienced the trauma of the hurricane itself, the flooded streets, the dangerous journey to higher ground, and eventually their rescue. Then they faced the anxiety of adjusting to a new place where they were strangers. At the point when we left the Walkers in the introduction, they had lived in Siloam Springs a few months, and though they were adapting to their new world, the children and Ruth were having some difficulty coping with their losses, adjustments, and memories. Ruth realized her family needed help with their traumatic memories, ongoing adjustments, and upcoming decisions.

So Ruth and her children joined a small group of other Katrina evacuees who met twice a month with a counselor. Over the next few months, Ruth's family learned to process how they felt about the hurricane and the trauma they had endured. They shared and they listened to each other. Some of those conversations follow:

Counselor (to James): How are you feeling about your time here in Siloam Springs?

James: It's okay, but we're going back home soon.

Counselor: What will you do in New Orleans?

James: Well, we'll go back to our apartment, and I'll go back to school and everything.

Counselor: How are you doing here in Siloam?

James: Okay, but it's not the same.

Counselor: What will be better in New Orleans?

James: We'll know everybody; I'll know the kids at school. I can be on my old soccer team.

Counselor: Anything else?

James: Well, our dad lives there, and maybe we could see him sometime.

Counselor: Do you expect him to come and visit you here, or help you get set up again in New Orleans?

Ruth: No, he has a new family—you kids know this. I expect he's taking care of them.

James: Yeah, but if we're there, we could see him maybe.

Counselor: Are you guys thinking you might go back to visit New Orleans and see what you can find in your old apartment?

Ruth: Well, we've talked about it a bit. Maybe we can go over spring break in March?

James: Yeah, and maybe things will be better there, and everything, and we can go back for good.

• • •

Counselor: Jada, do you have any questions about the time of the hurricane in New Orleans?

Jada (in a very small voice): I don't know what happened to my dollies.

Counselor: What do you think might have happened to them?

Jada (in an even smaller voice): I think they drowned-ed—because I lost them.

Counselor: Can you think of anything else that might have happened to them?

Jada: No, I think they drowned-ed.

Counselor: Do you think that maybe someone found your dollies?

Jada: Maybe, but we looked and we couldn't find them.

Counselor: What if someone else found your dollies?

Jada (looking up with hope on her face): Do you think so?

Counselor: What would they do if they found your dollies?

Jada: They would wash them and take good care of them.

Counselor: Maybe that's what happened. Maybe another little girl about your age found your dollies. Maybe she washed them and cleaned them up. Maybe she's hoping you are all right, and she wants you to know she's taking good care of your dollies. Would that be okay with you?

Jada: I think so . . . (and a sudden smile lit her face).

• • •

Counselor (to Terrell): How do you see your role in the family since the hurricane?

Terrell: Well, I think everybody is doing okay. James is liking his soccer team and likes his afterschool chess club. Jada loves her kindergarten teacher, and she likes sleeping in the same room with Mom. She's getting stronger and doesn't have nightmares as much as she used to. Mom is loving the choir and she got to sing a solo last week. We really like our church; it's like we already belonged there even the first week we came.

Counselor: And how are you?

Terrell: I'm good.

Counselor: What are you looking forward to?

Terrell: I will be able to get my driver's permit when I turn fifteen in a couple of months, and then I can start driving and help Mom with errands and stuff.

Counselor: Is there anything you're concerned about?

Terrell: Well, if it happens again, where will we go?

Counselor: How did you end up here in Siloam?

Terrell: I don't really know; I guess it was just where the buses were going.

Ruth: There were buses going to other places too. I thought Arkansas would be a good place for us. And it has been very good for us. I think

God has been watching over us, taking care of us, Terrell. You got to play football last fall and basketball this spring—something you always wanted to do, but you didn't think you would get to in New Orleans.

Terrell: Yeah, it's good.

Ruth: Terrell, you have been a great help to me as we got through Katrina and as we have made a place here, but you need to know God is taking care of us. We are going to be fine. And he is taking care of you.

Terrell: I know. (Terrell's eyes filled with tears as he turned his face away so no one would see.)

During spring break of 2006, the Walkers made a trip to New Orleans to see if they might be able to move back. Their apartment building was in dreadful shape. It was boarded up, but they were able to enter through a back door. Water had stood in their apartment for over a week in September, and everything they owned was completely ruined or had been stolen. The smell in the apartment was appalling, and they didn't stay long.

James was quiet, distraught. He had hoped they could come back and move in and everything would be okay. Of course, everywhere they went Jada looked for her pink backpack and her dollies. Terrell watched his mother and siblings closely, looking for a way to offer help or hope. They walked to the Johnsons' house and it was boarded up as well.

Nothing was the same; the schools weren't even open. Their dad was unable to meet them. Even James could see that there was nothing to come back to.

The Walkers traveled back to Siloam Springs, and on Labor Day weekend in September 2006, the Hurricane Katrina survivors met at the summer camp for a time of remembrance and gratitude. Again, people shared their stories of loss and survival and what they were doing now in Siloam. Then for a while they processed James's very first question: "Why did this happen to us?"

• • •

Ruth's family has experienced a great deal of loss, but they are each exhibiting an amazing amount of resilience. The resilience qualities, attitudes, and characteristics shared below have been fostered amid the child-self, child-others, and child-God relationships and in the spiritual conversations and insights.

- Ruth carried the weight of the trauma the family endured. Though Terrell also felt a strong sense of responsibility, Ruth bore the primary burden and covered her children, even Terrell.
- The family requested support from others, knowing they could not survive this ordeal alone.
- They found a new place to belong, and found new relationships.
- They learned to listen to each other, and each child's voice was heard—Terrell's concerns that another disaster could overtake them; James's need for the family to consider returning to New Orleans; Jada's fears about her dollies.
- They sought help in making meaning of their losses.
- They learned to express their hopes and fears.
- They acknowledged God's role in their survival and in their thriving.
- They leaned into hope.

There is one last episode to this story.

On May 22, 2011, Joplin, Missouri, was slammed with an EF-5 tornado that destroyed a huge swath of the city and killed 158 people. A week later, about a hundred people from Siloam Springs—volunteers from churches, city organizations, and a small Christian university—took several buses to Joplin to help with the massive cleanup. Among those volunteers were college sophomore Terrell, high school junior James, and seventh-grader Jada, along with their mom, newly minted registered nurse Ruth Walker.

When they arrived, they were given face masks and assigned tasks. James and Terrell joined a group of men spray-painting street names on the pavement, since all street signs were gone. They also painted house numbers in front of what remained of the homes in a several-block area. The whole time they helped with this task, James and Terrell talked of the hours they waded and rowed in the flooded streets of New Orleans; they remembered aloud their visit to their destroyed apartment, realizing that the children of Joplin would perhaps come back to their own houses to find memories of their shattered lives.

James said, "We're helping them find their houses, their stuff. I hope they find what they need to go on."

Terrell said, "Maybe we could invite them to Siloam!"

Ruth and Jada were part of a group of ten people who walked down a street that had already been "numbered." The organizers of the cleanup said the area had been guarded at night and that there had been no looters yet, so those with Ruth were asked to look through the area around each house, looking for identification, purses, and other things of value that could be claimed by homeowners. An area had been designated where found items could be labeled and later claimed. Ruth, Jada, and their group set to work, combing the area around the houses. Ruth found a wallet with a driver's license, social security card, and other important documents.

Under the rear concrete steps of a house that had been mostly blown away, Jada found a small yellow zippered case with five small dolls nestled in it. When Ruth, Jada, and their group reported back to the cleanup control center, Ruth turned in the wallet.

Jada asked if she could clean the little case and the dolls. She was shown an area with some sanitizer and wipes. Jada lovingly cleaned each doll and the small yellow case. Then she wrote a note that said, "I found your dollies. I took good care of them. They are waiting for you. Jada Walker."

The yellow case was marked and labeled, "For the little girl who lived at 1437 Grand Avenue, Joplin, MO."

Another sign of resilience is paying it forward. The Walkers are passing on what they have learned, helping those who have endured loss and trauma, and giving what they themselves have received.[1]

---

[1]I lived in Siloam Springs when the survivors of Hurricane Katrina arrived in our town, and I came to know some of them. The general parameters of the story are true: the 700 evacuees who arrived, the 150 volunteers who helped them at the Baptist Assembly Grounds, and the Joplin tornado. About 250 hurricane survivors did make Siloam Springs their home, and they were warmly welcomed by that caring community. Some of the hurricane survivors helped with the Joplin cleanup, as did my family. The Walker family's story is a composite of the experiences of Katrina survivors I met in Siloam along with the experiences of other survivors I read about in the newspaper and online.

This encouraging story of resilience highlights one of the unexpected findings in resilience literature—that resilience is not typically the result of extraordinary qualities or surprising interventions. Rather, children who make it usually have ordinary resources and protective factors in their lives.[2] Good support systems, strong relationships with caring adults, and a spirituality that entails faith, hope, and the belief that life has meaning can uphold and sustain children in the common troubles of life as well as the more serious adversities that may come. As adults, we are called to support the children around us in their journeys to wholeness in many ways, but especially as we nurture their relationships with themselves, with others, and with God. Let us embrace the role of being among the *ordinary* resources and protective factors in their lives.

---

[2]Masten, *Ordinary Magic*, 7.

Also by the Author

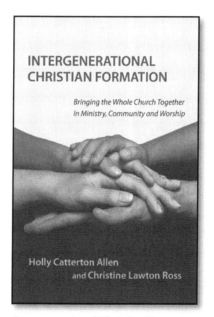

Intergenerational Christian Formation
978-0-8308-3981-0